CELEBRATION AND CHALLENGE

Fifty years of church teaching on education

and

Pope Francis' impact on renewal

JIM GALLAGHER SDB

Published June 2015

Salesians Farnborough Hampshire UK

Copyright Jim Gallagher SDB

Every effort has been made to seek permission for quotations. Any oversights in this area will be willingly remedied.

IN MEMORY

OF

HUBERT RICHARDS

AN OUTSTANDING SCRIPTURE SCHOLAR

AND

AN OUTSTANDING TEACHER

AND

PATRICK PURNELL S.J.

A TRULY INSPIRING FRIEND AND COLLEAGUE

Contents

Introduction   6

Chapters

1. The Vatican II declaration fifty years on.......... .10

2. The impact of Pope Francis on renewal............27

3. The Church's teaching since the council...........42

4. Current tensions and challenges.....................62

5. Recruiting and retaining teachers in schools.... 85

6. Pope Francis on educating for choosing life.....103

7. Benedict XVI's visit to Britain.......................121

8. Pope Francis and Don Bosco on education......132

9. Some Conclusions and quality marks 146

10. Why does the Catholic Church have schools 150.

Appendix

INTRODUCTION

2015 is for me a special year, a year of celebration. It is fifty years since the close of Vatican II and fifty years since the Council's Declaration on Christian Education was finally approved on 28th October 1965. We also celebrate twenty five years of the Apostolic Constitution Ex Corde Ecclesiae on Catholic universities. 2015 is also the year in which we celebrate the bicentenary of the birth of St. John Bosco, patron of youth and the founder of my own religious congregation, the Salesians of Don Bosco, on 16th August. Don Bosco was an inspirational and innovative educator and Salesian schools, youth centres, missions for street kids and marginalised young people are to be found in every continent.

1965 was my first year in Rome as a young student of theology. It was an exciting year in which I heard some thought provoking talks by some of the leading thinkers at the Council. I was privileged to be present in St. Peter's at a number of the voting sessions and particularly at the final session which approved the Pastoral Constitution on the Church in the Modern World, Gaudium et Spes. On that occasion I managed to secure a seat close to the papal altar in the left transept with a clear view of the figure of Don Bosco surrounded by a group of young people, in the niche right above the famous statue of St. Peter. Every time I return to Rome I find that spot, my sacred spot, and rededicate myself to Vatican II and Don Bosco. I was also present with a fellow student at the very moving closing Mass in St. Peter's Square where we found ourselves, by some good fortune and a little guile, in the front row with a great view of the pope, the cardinals and bishops. I was then a young student filled with the hope of the New Pentecost that seemed to be beginning in the aftermath of the Council, the greatest religious event of the twentieth century.

After Rome I did further studies in education and catechesis and all my priestly life I have worked in these fields in different roles and with different responsibilities: Head of R.E, in what is now Savio Salesian College, Bootle, Senior Lecturer in theology and R.E. in Liverpool Institute of Higher Education (now Hope University), Co-ordinator of the National Project of Catechesis and Religious Education, Living and Sharing Our Faith, Bishops' Conference, and later Adviser (Religious Dimension) for the twenty Catholic Secondary schools in the diocese of Shrewsbury. At the same time I had responsibilities in my own Salesian province. As Co-ordinator of the National Project I was privileged to work with Fr. Patrick Purnell and Brother Damian Lundy, both outstanding in the fields of catechesis and religious education, from whom I learnt a great deal. As well as working in consultation with Diocesan Advisers preparing resources for schools and parishes, I addressed and had lively discussions with many groups in various dioceses. I was deeply impressed by the hard work of catechists and teachers, and the dedication of Diocesan Advisers to the mission of helping teachers, catechists and parishioners to understand and commit themselves to the vision of Vatican II. It was an exciting and demanding time. It is this experience of meeting, addressing and learning from these people, especially school staff, senior leadership teams, and governors, that is the background or context which I have in mind as I write this text.

The hope I and many had in 1965 faded somewhat in the 80s and 90s but has now been rekindled and celebrated anew with the election of Pope Francis and the spirit of hope which he preaches in his words and actions. It is my hope that more experienced teachers and the new generation of teachers in our Catholic schools will recommit or commit themselves to the vision of the God-given dignity of all people, our students and their families, and the wonder of our world, God's world, spelt out in the documents of Vatican II. In order to achieve this I offer this fairly brief text by way of inspiration and challenge with some key quotations from the Declaration of the Council, some of the documents on schools of the Congregation for Catholic Education, especially the latest marking the occasion of the fiftieth anniversary. I also include reflections of Pope Francis on Catholic education expressed to teachers in Argentina in his book *Education for Choosing Life: Proposals for Difficult Times*. I dedicate a chapter with some thoughts on Don Bosco's system of education in this bicentenary year of his birth and Pope Francis's thoughts addressed to the Salesian General Chapter, as well as a chapter on reflections of Benedict XVI on education during his successful visit to Britain.

I present these quotations and reflections as inspiration and challenge to all involved and interested in the mission of our schools and particularly to those with responsibilities for our schools: head teachers, senior leadership teams, teachers, all staff, chaplains, governors, parents and parish priests. It is my hope that these reflections and radical quotations will encourage personal and group reflections in school briefings and in-service days; I also hope that they may enable all of us to be more convinced of the value of our schools and help us to see how irreplaceable they are within the mission of the Church in today's Britain.[1] The fiftieth anniversary of the Vatican II Declaration on Christian Education seems a good time to take up the challenge.

Jim Gallagher SDB

Farnborough Hampshire

June 2015

---

[1] See my article *Are Our Schools Irreplaceable?*, Pastoral Review, Jan/Feb 2010

Chapter One

THE VATICAN II DECLARATION FIFTY YEARS ON

> *In the years following the Second Vatican Council, Papal Magisterium has repeatedly insisted on the importance of education in general, as well as on the contribution that the Christian community is called to offer education. Therefore, the anniversaries of 2015 are a suitable and invaluable opportunity for taking on board the recommendations of the Education Magisterium and sketching out guidelines for the coming decades.* [2]

> *It must never be forgotten that the school is always in the process of being created due to the labour brought to fruition by all who have a role to play in it, and most especially by those who are teachers.* [3]

In 2015 we keep the fiftieth anniversary of the Vatican II's Declaration on Christian Education – a veritable landmark. The Congregation for Catholic Education has issued a document *Educating Today and Tomorrow: A Renewing Passion* to help us recall and celebrate the occasion and respond to the challenges with the aim 'to give new stimulus to the Church's involvement in the

---

[2] Congregation for Catholic Education, Educating Today and Tomorrow: A renewing Passion, 2014. The page references are taken from the downloaded test.

[3] Lay Catholics in School n. 78

field of education'. While this document is addressed principally to Bishops' Conferences, 'the text is also addressed to national and international association of teachers, parents, students and former students as well as associations of those who run schools and universities'; it is also addressed 'to Christian communities so that they may reflect on the importance of Catholic education in the context of New Evangelisation'. Really it is for a wide audience of people who take seriously the future of Catholic education and the survival and development of our schools. It is my hope that this text might make this document and others of the Congregation for Catholic Education more readily accessible to all who are involved and interested in Catholic education particularly in our schools. The texts of these documents encourage us to reflect on the challenges, and they are many, which our schools now face and will continue to face in the years ahead. At the same time they invite us to acknowledge the very real success stories of the renewal called for by Vatican II and to celebrate them without in any way giving into complacency. This most recent document included a questionnaire which was intended to help individuals and groups 'to provide indications, suggestions and proposals' for consideration at the Global Convention which will be held in Rome 18-21 November 2015. Responses were to be sent to Rome by 31 July 2014! Some readers may have been involved in discussions or invited to respond through schools or in dioceses and parishes. Others may not have heard of the document of the Congregation for Catholic Education or may be unaware that 2015 is the fiftieth anniversary of the Vatican II Declaration on Christian Education.

A new stimulus to our involvement in education

The reason for writing this text is to help ensure that the fiftieth anniversary of the Declaration on Christian Education does not go unnoticed and to try to make the Vatican document marking the occasion, as well as some of the post-conciliar documents on Catholic education, more readily accessible to head teachers, senior leadership teams, teachers, parents, students, to governors and Christian communities which should be interested in and prepared to defend vigorously with well thought out reasons for our right to have Catholic schools and our confidence in their value for the wider community, not just for the Church. Most of these people, teachers and others, will be busy with many duties whether in school, home or parish or in other tasks which make it difficult to find the time to read, reflect on and discuss the points raised in the documents and take any necessary action. It would certainly be a great shame if such a document and the others urging us to give serious thought to Catholic education should go unnoticed or unmarked by the many people who are involved in Catholic education in our schools at this time of the fiftieth year, the Golden Jubilee, of the Council's Declaration.

This is a time when our schools are continually under fierce attack especially by hostile and vociferous humanist and secular associations, and by some within the Church for the schools' apparent failure in 'passing on the faith'; at a time when the Government continues to pass legislation which too often enshrines poorly thought-out changes in educational policy, and when there may well be problems and tensions with Local Authorities and others. The latest Vatican document states quite clearly that it can and should be used 'to effect a pastoral evaluation of this area of the Church's mission in the context of New Evangelisation'. The document recalls the fundamental characteristics of Catholic schools and describes the challenges to which Catholic schools and universities are called to respond bearing in mind 'the development of their own specific mission'. As I have already mentioned, while our schools seek to provide a sound Christian holistic education, they do so in the context of a constant bombardment of changes in the Government's educational policy and of the general disquiet with inspections and how they judge and grade what makes a 'good', an 'outstanding school', a 'failing school'. While the Vatican document is addressed to the world-wide Catholic community and offers recommendations and guidelines, I shall address those challenges and tensions which seem more relevant to our situation and to 'the development of our own specific mission' in the multi-cultural, multi-religious and secular society of Britain today. Reflection and discussion of such issues should inspire and challenge us to be faithful to the true aim of Catholic education in the context of changes in culture:

> Contemporary culture is affected by several problems that are causing a widespread 'educational emergency': this expression refers to

the difficulty in establishing educational relationships which, in order to be genuine, should convey vital values and principles to younger generations, not only to help individual growth but also to contribute to building the common good.[4]

Clearly when speaking of widespread 'educational emergency' the document refers in a special way to the difficulty of creating a climate of warm and mutual educational relationships between teachers and students in which schools can pass on to our young people the values and principles which are the outstanding, distinctive marks of the true Catholic and human education we seek to provide and which will enable young people 'to contribute to building the common good'. Much is made of this important issue in the document and the thoughts of Pope Francis and will be consider in the following chapters.

The Declaration on Christian Education part of the overall message of the Council

The Declaration of Vatican II, *Gravissimum Educationis*, does not stand alone it is part of the overall message of Vatican II and, as the recent Vatican document states, 'should be considered within the Council's overall teachings and read together with other texts approved by the Council'. Some of the Council documents have a clear relationship to the education we seek to provide in our schools. The Constitution on Liturgy has particular

---

[4] Educating Today and Tomorrow: A Renewing Passion, introduction.

importance within schools in the celebration of Masses on special occasions and in services which mark the Church's liturgical year, all to be suitably adapted to meet the needs of the age groups and encourage participation of the primary pupils and the older students. The Pastoral Constitution *Gaudium et Spes*, the Church in the Modern World, has much to offer in its analysis of faith and culture, the condition of humanity in the modern world, and with its clarion call to all involved in education and pastoral care of the young:

> We can justly consider that the future lies in the hands of those who are strong enough to provide coming generations with reasons for living and hoping.[5]

In the Decree on the Apostolate of Lay People there is a renewed understanding and appreciation of the role and vocation of lay people within the Church and particularly in the field of education. This is further developed in the document published by the Congregation for Catholic Education in 1982 *Lay Catholics: Witnesses to Faith.*

> It is the lay teachers, and indeed all lay persons, believers or not, who will substantially determine whether or not the school realises its aims and accomplishes its objectives. In the Declaration on Christian Education the Church recognised the role and responsibility that this situation confers on all those lay Catholics who work in any type of elementary and secondary schools, whether as

---

[5] Pastoral Constitution *Gaudium et Spes*, n. 55

teachers, directors, administrators or auxiliary staff.[6]

Increasing importance must also now be given to the *Decree on Ecumenism*, the Declarations on Religious Liberty and on the Relation of the Church to Non-Christian Religions. These have taken on special relevance in our multi-cultural, multi-faith and secular society. They now make new demands on teaching staff as they seek to encourage students to have mutual respect for all people, to engage in sincere dialogue according to their situation, age and abilities, to live as neighbours with others of different faiths and cultures. We educate in order to enable the young eventually to play a fully human and Christian role in ensuring social cohesion among different groups and in contributing to the common good of all in our multi-faith, multi-cultural, secular society. This is the theme of the 2013 document of the Vatican Congregation Educating to Intercultural Dialogue in Catholic Schools: Living in Harmony for a Civilisation of Love.

> Schools have a great responsibility in this field, called as they are to develop intercultural dialogue in their pedagogical vision. This is a difficult goal, not easy to achieve, and yet it is necessary. Education, by its nature, requires both openness to other cultures, without the loss of one's own identity, and an acceptance of the other person, to avoid the risk of limited culture, closed in on itself.[7]

---

[6] *Lay Catholics in Schools: Witnesses to Faith*, introduction.

[7] *Educating to Intercultural Dialogue in Catholic Schools*, introduction.

This joint reading of the Council and other post-conciliar documents helps us 'appreciate the two dimensions that education necessarily encompasses, when it is being analysed from the standpoint of faith: the secular and theological-spiritual dimensions'[8]. Unfortunately many of us do not have the luxury of the time needed to reread the various documents of Vatican II and of the rich educational and theological documents published by the Vatican Congregation in the years since the Council. Those who are engaged in further study such as a Masters in Catholic Education and other courses will have the opportunity to read and reflect on them. More educators should be encouraged to apply for such courses which are essential for those who aspire to leadership responsibilities within our schools. However, it is the task of all involved in education in our schools to ensure that these dimensions are an essential aspect of what we do in schools with our primary pupils and secondary students. As Pope Francis reminds us 'at the very heart of the Gospel is life in community and engagement with others'[9]

In this text I shall reflect on those issues which I see as more relevant to the situation we face. I cannot and make no attempt to cover all the points raised in a document addressed to the world-wide Catholic community. My main focus will be on the text of this latest document of the Congregation for Catholic Education, *Educating Today and Tomorrow: A Renewing Passion*, with its consideration of 'current and future educational

---

[8] *Educating Today and Tomorrow* p.5

[9] *Evangelii Gaudium* n. 117

challenges' and the documents of the Congregation for Catholic Education which followed the Council. I shall attempt to comment on their relevance to my own experience and those of teachers and students which I have been privileged to meet and know.

Pope Francis and his call for personal and pastoral conversion

I am very conscious of doing this in the hopeful context of Pope Francis and his call for renewal in the Church. Right from the start of his pontificate Pope Francis has proposed a model of Church in harmony with the great proposals of Vatican II. He calls for 'personal and pastoral conversion' and does so with exquisite pastoral sensitivity. We undertake this response to 'a pastoral ministry in a missionary style' in the context of Pope Francis' call for renewal as spelt out in his Apostolic Exhortation *Evangelii Gaudium*, his mission statement for a Church which is very aware of God's love and mercy and shows such love and mercy towards all, especially the poor and marginalised. In his exhortation the pope declares:

> The Second Vatican Council presented ecclesial conversion as openness to a constant self-renewal born of fidelity to Jesus Christ: every renewal of the Church consists in an increase of fidelity to her own calling...Christ summons the Church as she goes her pilgrim way...to that continual reformation of which she has always need, as so far as she is a human institution here on earth.

> I dream of a 'missionary option', that is a missionary impulse capable of transforming everything, so that the Church's customs, ways of doing things, times and schedules, language and structures can be suitably channelled for evangelisation of today's world rather than her self-preservation. [10]

Such is the 'dream' of Pope Francis and one which he sees becoming a reality in the world through our fidelity to Jesus the Christ and the 'missionary impulse' which takes account of the real circumstances in which people find themselves. It is a message which he frequently reiterates. While this applies to all we do in the world as Christians in spreading the Good News of God's Kingdom, it must surely apply to our mission in Catholic schools in which through education we also evangelise and look outward to the needs of people in our world and not simply to our own self-preservation and self-interest. Such is 'new evangelisation': fidelity to Jesus and his teaching and way of life and sincere attention to the concerns, anxieties and real needs of people, especially the young in the cultural situation of today. This is the Catholic school's mission.

The pope stresses three important aspects of education

In his address to the participants in the plenary session of the Congregation for Catholic Education in February

---

[10] Evangelii Gaudium n. 26 & 27

2014 Pope Francis declared 'Catholic education is one of the most important challenges for the Church, committed today to carrying out the New Evangelisation in an historical and cultural context in constant transformation'. He then went on to propose three aspects for special consideration: a) the value of dialogue in education; b) the qualified preparation of teachers; c) the responsibilities of Catholic schools and universities to express the living presence of the Gospel in the fields of education, science and culture.

Dialogue in education

With regard to the value of dialogue in education, he made reference to the document published in 2013 by the Congregation Educating to Intercultural Dialogue in *Catholic Schools: Living in Harmony for a Civilisation of Love.* He went on to say that Catholic schools and universities are frequented by many non-Christian students and non-believers.

> The Catholic institutions offer to all an educational proposal that looks to the integral development of the person and that responds to the right of all to accede to learning and knowledge and using the methods appropriate to the school environment the Christian proposal, namely Jesus as the meaning of life, of the cosmos and of history'.

He expressed his appreciation for those who run schools in 'contexts of accentuated cultural and religious pluralism'.

The profound changes that have led to the ever greater diffusion of multi-cultural societies asks all of those who operate in the school and university sector to involve themselves in educational itineraries of encounter and dialogue, with courageous and innovative fidelity which will be able to make the Catholic identity meet with different 'spirits' of the multi-cultural society.

This clearly has particular relevance in some countries of the world but it is also a tension and challenge which we are facing more and more in our multi-cultural society and schools today and one which I will consider again when we discuss the challenges set out in this latest Vatican document. The pope's words challenge us not to cut ourselves off in a closed Catholic context but to undertake 'educational itineraries and dialogue with courageous and innovative fidelity' in engaging others different from ourselves. On this the pope is very strong.

Teacher preparation

The second aspect regards the 'qualified preparation of educators'. It seems best to use Pope Francis' own words which we will consider in greater depth later.

> In the meeting I had with the General Superiors, I stressed that today education is addressed to a generation that changes; therefore, every educator – and the whole Church which is Mother Educator - is called to change, in the sense of being able to communicate with the young people she has

before her...To educate is an act of love. It is to give life. And love is demanding it calls for using the best resources... The educator in Catholic schools must be, first and foremost, very competent, qualified, and at the same time rich in humanity...Because of this the educator is in need of permanent formation'.

He stresses the need 'of permanent formation' because of the fast changing world in which we and the young are caught up in and acknowledges that this is of the utmost importance if we really wish to communicate with the young well versed as they are in the use of the latest social media. We should make great efforts to respect and understand them. He reminds us that 'to educate is an act of love, it is to give life', and love makes great demands on all who take up this vocation and mission. The dedicated teacher, according to Pope Francis, must be 'competent, qualified, and rich in humanity'. This has a good deal to say to us about the recruitment and induction of new staff. He insists that in this matter 'We cannot improvise. We must engage'. The recruitment and retention of staff for our schools and suitable initial induction for new teachers, the on-going professional training for teachers who have been in the school for some time are some of the major responsibilities and challenges facing us today. We shall consider this in other chapters.

Living presence of Gospel in education

With regard to the third important aspect, the Pope makes reference to the responsibilities of schools and universities to express the living presence of the Gospel in the field of education, of science and of culture: 'Catholic institutions must not be isolated from the world; they must be able to enter with courage in the Areopagus of present-day cultures and engage in dialogue, aware of the gift they have to offer everyone'. The Areopagus is a reference to the section in the Acts of the Apostles, chapter 17, where Paul preaches on the hill in Athens, the Areopagus, and instead of berating the Athenians in anger, his initial reaction being one of disgust - 'his whole soul was revolted the city given over to idolatry', he praises them for their religious care of the altar of the unknown god and he goes on to tell them that is the One he is there to speak of. He seeks and makes use of positive values in what is an alien culture. That is what Pope Francis asks of us in education today 'aware of the gift' we have to offer. He constantly reminds us that such an offer should be made with gentleness and respect.

Constant evaluation and return to basic principles

In the aftermath of the Council the Vatican Congregation has published a number of documents which have inspired us to keep re-evaluating what we do in schools as we recall basic principles. I shall continue to refer to some of these texts. I quote from them quite a lot in my previous book on Catholic schools[11]. At this point I quote two which are still very relevant, even more so today, and speak of the tensions and challenges which are

---

[11] *Serving the Young: Our Catholic Schools Today*, Don Bosco Publications.

constantly with us. Firstly the 1977 document of the Congregation written within ten years of the Council.

> One must recognise that more than ever before, the job of the Catholic school is infinitely more difficult, more complex, since this is a time when Christianity demands to be clothed in new garments. When all manner of changes have been introduced in the Church and in secular life, and particularly, when a pluralist mentality dominates and the Christian Gospel is increasingly pushed to the side lines. It is because of this that loyalty to the educational aims of the Catholic school demands constant self-evaluation and return to basic principles, to the motives which inspire the Church's involvement in education.[12]

Secondly I quote the 1997 document issued at the turn of the century.

> Young people can be found again among those who have lost all sense of the meaning in life and lack any type of inspiring ideal, those to whom no values are proposed and who do not know the beauty of faith, who come from families which are broken and incapable of love, often living in situations of material and spiritual poverty, slaves to the new idols of society which not infrequently, promises them only a future of unemployment and marginalisation. To these new poor the Catholic school turns in a spirit of love by offering the

---

[12] *The Catholic School* n 66-67

opportunity for education, for training for a job, of human and Christian formation. [13]

We can recognise this as the situation of many of our students particularly, but not only, among those from more deprived areas of Britain; a large percentage of these young people are in our schools with their particular anxieties and needs. Here is a great rallying cry which is surely close to the heart of Pope Francis and what he 'dreams' for the pastoral mission of the Church: 'to these new poor the Catholic school turns in a spirit of love'. I shall reflect on these in the light of what is expressed in the various Church documents from the Vatican, from the reflections of Pope Francis and from our own Bishops' Conference over the last fifty years.

In the spirit of Pope Francis it is also a time for hope and joy, for celebration.

> Challenges exist to be overcome! Let us be realistic, but without losing our joy, our boldness and our hope-filled commitment. Let us not allow ourselves to be robbed of missionary vigour. [14]

---

[13] *The Catholic School on the Threshold of the Third Millennium* n.15

[14] *Evangelii Gaudium* n.65.

PAUSE FOR REFLECTION

Does the school have any plans for marking the 50th anniversary of the Declaration on Christian Education with staff, students, Governors and others who have an interest in Catholic education?

Is the diocese planning to make use of this anniversary by special days for staff and Governors? Are some members of your staff planning to take part?

In what ways do the pope's important points speak to you: a) the value of dialogue in education, b) the qualified preparation of teachers, c) expressing the presence of the Gospel in the fields of education, science and culture?

How could the document be used to effect a pastoral evaluation of this area of the Church's mission by the local Catholic community – the schools and parishes?

Chapter Two

THE IMPACT OF POPE FRANCIS ON RENEWAL

I am aware that nowadays documents do not arouse the same interest as in the past and that they are quickly forgotten. Nevertheless, I want to emphasise that what I am trying to express here has a programmatic significance and important consequences. I hope that all communities will devote the necessary effort to advancing along the path of pastoral and missionary conversion which cannot leave things as they presently are.[15]

Catholic education is one of the most important challenges of the Church, committed today to carrying out the New Evangelisation in an historic and cultural context in constant transformation.[16]

Pope Francis has in a fairly short time made a great impression by his words and above all by his actions not only on Catholics, but on Christians of different denomination, on those of other faiths and on those who do not profess any religious faith. His appeal is fairly universal. We admire his simple life style, his living in the Sancta Marta Guest House, eating and meeting with the other residents and guests rather than living alone in the

---

[15] Evangelii Gaudium n.25

[16] Pope Francis address to the Congregation for Catholic Education, February 2014

relative splendour of the Vatican apartments. He features frequently in the press and on television. The photographs in the newspapers and magazines of his being with children, the young, the elderly, the sick and disabled, prisoners, the marginalised speak to us of his warm, compassionate love for people, of his openness to all. We see a man who not only speaks of the compassion and mercy of God but who bears living witness to it. At the same time he is seeking to undertake necessary reforms in the Church fully aware that we 'cannot leave things as they presently are' and he does so in a robust and open way that is pastoral and sensitive: 'advancing along the path of pastoral and missionary conversion'.

> Pope Francis has presented himself as a new breath of the Spirit blowing on the Church, slimming down its bureaucracy, making the Church poorer and more simple, and above all urging it to go out into the world's highways and byways to evangelise. He has made us feel that the Church is a Mother filled with tenderness and love, filled with kindness, humility, patience. He has taught this through his gestures, attitudes and personal choices, his way of relating to the world. [17]

I for one am greatly encouraged and challenged by all he says and does and feel sure that many others are. There is much in what he says, particularly in his Apostolic Exhortation *Evangelii Gaudium,* and his other reflections, and in his whole attitude to people in different situations

---

[17] P. Chavez Villaneuva, former Rector Major, address at 27th General Chapter of the Salesians

which speaks powerfully to all of us who have the responsibilities for the pastoral care of pupils, students, their parents, of all staff and of the local and wider community.

Evangelii Gaudium sets out his vision

At the beginning of *Evangelii Gaudium* he sets out the themes and questions which he wishes to discuss at length, among these are the reform of the Church in her missionary outreach, the temptations faced by pastoral workers, the inclusion of the poor, peace and dialogue within society.

> I have dealt extensively with these topics, with a detail which some may find exhaustive. But I have done so, not with the intention of providing an exhaustive treatise but simply as a way of showing their important practical implications for the Church's mission today. All of them give shape to a definite style of evangelisation which I ask you to adopt in every activity which you undertake. [18]

Such themes have practical implications for the mission we undertake as educators and evangelisers of the young faced often with the temptation to question, even despair of the good we do and achieve in the life of the school, of the care we give to the poor and of our ability to dialogue with and even understand those indifferent to religion or antagonistic to it. All of this is essentially linked with

---

[18] *Evangelii Gaudium* n.18'

evangelisation. In our Catholic schools we evangelise by educating.

> Catholic schools which always strive to join their work of education with the explicit proclamation of the Gospel, are a most valuable source for evangelisation of culture, even in those countries and cities where hostile situations challenge us to greater creativity in our search for suitable methods. [19]

For many teachers, especially some who are not Catholic and indeed some who may be Catholic, such language and terms – 'explicit proclamation of the Gospel and evangelisation' - may well be somewhat strange and off putting. As we shall see, Pope Francis is very sensitive to the language we use as we proclaim the Gospel and its implications for all we do for our students and staff in our Catholic schools. The pope speaks of the need to understand why people may find such language somewhat off-putting and have an impression of a rather crude style of Bible preaching on the need for conversion and salvation. He inculcates a more missionary approach in our language and attitude. The pope reminds all of those in the educating community of our schools that we educate with

> ...the sole object of training and helping to develop mature people who are simple, competent and honest, and know how to love with fidelity, who can live life as a response to God's call, and their future profession as a service to society. [20]

---

[19] op. cit. n.134

Such is in large part the message of the Gospel and of evangelisation.

The Pope who was a teacher

We have a Pope who has been a teacher. In the 1960s and 70s he taught literature and psychology to young students in Jesuit schools in Buenos Aires and Santa Fe. Later he was also a professor at the San Miguel School of Theology. As Pope he has addressed various groups of students and teachers and those involved in education and told them that he loved school and had fond memories of many of his teachers. He addressed over 300,000 students, their families and teachers gathered in St. Peter's square to celebrate the 'Church for Schools Day' organised by the Italian bishops. On that occasion he mentioned in particular his first teacher in the first grade when he was six years old: 'I have never forgotten her. She is why I loved school. I visited her throughout her life until she passed away aged 98'. A past student rated him highly as a teacher who guided students through the subject material 'with suggestions and explanations rather than like the typical teacher, who orchestrates and dictates'. He shored up their self-confidence. He says 'the students always went to Fr. Bergolio for help and support; we knew we could tell him any kind of problem and be absolutely certain that he would help us find a solution'. He tells of a group of students who wanted to form a Beatles cover band. Bit by bit, with the support of Fr. Bergolio, the students got

---

[20] Address to the Jesuit Schools of Italy and Albania

hold of the instruments, sound equipment and sheet music.

The student was very appreciative of the priest's good relationship with his parents since he was a bit of unruly adolescent.[21] Clearly the Pope has experienced the joys and trials of the teacher. As a Jesuit and an Archbishop he has written extensively on education. We have his inspiring and challenging talks and discussions with Argentinian teachers in his book Education for Choosing Life: Proposals for Difficult Times. I shall discuss this more fully in a later chapter. He is very much aware of the rapid and on-going changes in education that are constantly taking place and of the demands made on teachers and the pressure of the 'production of/by results' on students and teachers. He acknowledges that teachers are frequently undervalued by many in society and not given the respect due to those who undertake this essential vocation and mission in the name of society and the Church. He frequently speaks on these issues.

Dialogue in education in our pluralist society

As I have already pointed out, in his address to the Congregation for Catholic Education in February 2014 he declared 'Catholic education is one of the most important challenges of the Church'. He spoke of the challenges which Catholic schools face in addressing the needs of students and teachers in today's multi-cultural, multi-ethnic, multi-religious, non- believing society. In Catholic

---

[21] J. Milia, Catholic News Service 12 March 2014

educational institutes throughout the world he acknowledges that besides Catholics with a variety of practise and commitment, there are a number, often quite a large number, of other Christians, of 'non-Christians and even non-believers' and he clearly declares that 'full respect for each one's dignity must be respected'. This applies of course to our students; it also applies to members of staff of which as many as 45% in secondary schools and some 20% in primary schools are not Catholic. In this regard he stresses the need for what he calls 'the value of dialogue in education'. Dialogue is a word he frequently uses and finds inspiration for this in the fact that 'Jesus proclaimed the Good News in Galilee of the Gentiles: a crossroads of persons of different races, culture and religion'[22]. Jesus left his home town of Nazareth and moved to the larger, more cosmopolitan town of Capernaum to begin his ministry, in a town where there were a great diversity of people of different races, cultures and religion. He sees similarities to our own situation today and once again he calls on those responsible for Catholic education not to close themselves in a Catholic world but to enter into respectful dialogue with others as Paul did on the hill of the Areopagus when addressing the Athenians in their alien, antagonistic culture.

The question of neutrality in education

These developments demand of us a radical examination of the purpose of our schools and of how we may best

---

[22] Pope Francis, Address to the Congregation for Catholic Education 2014

articulate and give our reasons for such a purpose to others in a way that is attractive and compelling. We will not satisfy all our critics especially the very vocal and hostile who hold an out and out secularist view such as that expressed by the National Secular Society. They maintain that the promotion and public funding of religious schools to be divisive and detrimental to social cohesion. State funding of religious schools for them is the least appropriate response to this diversity. They would like to see steps taken to ensure children of all faiths and none are educated together in a respectful but religiously neutral environment.

We have to ask what is meant by a 'religiously neutral environment', a secular environment, how 'neutral' is that? In a sense there is really no such thing as 'neutrality' since we all have our beliefs and convictions about what is important in our understanding about life. While not imposing such beliefs and convictions on others, we cannot simply leave them aside as we seek to educate our students for life. The 1997 Vatican document reminds us that 'there is a tendency to forget that education always proposes and involves a definite concept of the person and life'.

> To claim neutrality for schools signifies in practice, more times than not, banning all reference to religion from the cultural and educational field, whereas a correct pedagogical approach ought to be open to the more decisive sphere of ultimate objectives, attending not only to how but also why, overcoming any misunderstanding as regards the neutrality in education, restoring to the

educational process the unity which saves it from dispersion amid the meandering of knowledge and acquired facts, and focuses on the human person in his or her integral, transcendent, historic identity. [23]

That is why inspired by the Gospel the Catholic school takes up this challenge always respecting individual freedom and choice. There are many keen and dedicated teachers and others who are prepared to share our goal of integrated, holistic education especially if we try to find the right language that speaks to people who are defined before all else by their responsibility to their sisters and brothers.

Finding the right language which appeals to people

Pope Francis challenges us to give careful thought to the language we use and of the way we communicate the message: 'we need to be realistic and not assume that our audience understands the full background to what we are saying, or is capable of relating what we say to the very heart of the Gospel which gives it meaning, beauty and attractiveness'. He then goes on to say that we need to take up a missionary approach or style.

> Pastoral ministry in a missionary style is not obsessed with the disjointed transmission of a multitude of doctrines to be insistently imposed. When we adopt a pastoral goal and missionary

---

[23] *The Catholic School on the Threshold of the Third Millennium* nn.9&10

style which would actually reach everyone without exemption or exclusion, the message has to concentrate on the essentials, on what is most beautiful, most grand, most appealing and at the same time necessary. The message is simplified, while losing none of its depth and truth, and thus becomes all the more forceful and convincing. [24]

This applies to all preaching of the Good News and he speaks a good deal of this in his *Evangelii Gaudium*. We must surely apply it to the way we articulate and defend the value and importance of our Catholic schools and the education we seek to provide. For Francis style and language are very important. As the pope says 'we have to try to make the central point of our activities the integral formation of the person, that is to say, the contribution to the full maturation of free and responsible men and women'[25]. Our aim should be 'the full maturation of free and responsible men and women'. This is a constant theme stated forcefully in a number of Vatican documents.

> The purpose of instruction at school is education: the development of persons from within, freeing them from that conditioning which prevents them from becoming fully integrated human beings. The school's educational programme is intentionally directed to the growth of the whole person.[26]

---

[24] *Evangelii Gaudium* n. 35

[25] J. M. Bergoglio, *Education for Choosing Life*, Ignatius Press, San Francisco p. II1

[26] *The Catholic School* n.29

Every school, and every educator in the school, ought to be striving to form strong and responsible individuals, who are capable of making free and correct choices', thus preparing young people 'to open themselves more and more to reality, and to form in themselves a clear idea of the meaning of life. [27]

An educating community challenged and inspired by the Gospel

Not many educators would disagree or find fault with such statements of intent even if they cannot fully adhere to the faith vision which underpins them. A good number of teachers and others happily play a constructive, supporting role in the educating communities of our schools. It is, however, vitally important that we continue to spell out clearly and unambiguously the true aim of all that we do in our schools through the ethos we seek to create, as well as the teaching and learning and the many other activities in the life of the school that it is essentially focused on the human flourishing of all our students – and indeed our teachers. We do so inspired by our faith vision in the unique value of each person created in the image God. As Pope Francis says, we cannot simply assume that all will fully understand and appreciate our educational aims 'relating all we say to the very heart of the Gospel'. For this reason he constantly reminds us that in such situations we must be open to dialogue and take a more pastoral and missionary

---

[27] *Lay Catholics in Schools* n.17; the quotations *are from The Catholic school* n.31

approach which seeks to understand and respect the views of others while expressing clearly our own vision of education. He says

> It is true that in our dealing with the world, we are told to give reasons for hope, but not as an enemy who critiques and condemns...but with gentleness and reverence. [28]

We set out our position as one of Christian humanism: we believe in the dignity of every person founded on our belief in creation and incarnation and we seek to develop the human person to his or her full potential. The pope urges us to concentrate 'on the essential, what is most beautiful, most grand, most appealing and at the same time necessary' which should ensure that the message 'becomes all the more forceful and convincing'. This is a great challenge for us in the context of our post-modern culture and the fairly wide-spread anti-religious feeling or indifference to religion and the over reliance on the media for values and ideas about religion, the Church and many other institutions. These are challenges for families and for schools.

> We are all aware of the ever mounting difficulties that hinder us from walking beside our children outside our educational institutions. As I told you in the forum, the pressures of the market, with its offerings of consumption and ruthless competition, the lack of economic, social, psychological, and moral resources, the even greater gravity of the risks to be avoided...all that makes it an uphill

---

[28] *Evangelii Gaudium* n.271

battle for families to fulfil their function, and makes schools even more isolated in the task of containing, sustaining and promoting the human development of their students. [29]

We are all very conscious of these difficulties and obstacles to what we seek to achieve in our mission with young people and their families. Yet despite all the difficulties we face, Pope Francis is optimistic if we face these challenges with courage and fortitude and he takes heart in the fact that

> Despite the tide of secularism which has swept our societies, the Catholic Church is considered a credible institution by public opinion and, trusted for her solidarity and concern for those in greatest need…And how much good has been done by our schools and universities around the world! This is a good thing. [30]

Pope Francis acknowledges the good that is being done while encouraging us to face the very real challenges which we face in supporting and developing our schools. Therefore, we can and should celebrate the good we do and achieve through our schools, while being very aware of the many challenges and tensions and striving to address them responsibly and courageously.

---

[29] Education for Choosing Life p.87-88

[30] Evangelii Gaudium n.65

PAUSE FOR REFLECTION

Has Pope Francis impressed you, your friends, your students; in what ways?

What impact do you think he is having on the Church?

Pope Francis challenges us to give careful thought to the language we use and the way we communicate the message; how necessary do you think this is when we try to explain the reasons for our Catholic schools?

Do you disagree with the humanists and others that our schools are detrimental to social coherence? Do you agree with Pope Francis that our schools do much good? What reasons and proof can you give?

Chapter Three
THE CHURCH'S TEACHING ON EDUCATION SINCE THE COUNCIL

> *The Holy Synod hereby promulgates some fundamental principles concerning Christian education, especially in regard to schools. These principles should be more fully developed by a special post-conciliar commission and should be adapted to different local circumstances by episcopal conferences.* [31]

> *I invite everyone to be bold and creative in this task of rethinking the goals, structures, style and methods of evangelisation in their respective communities...The important thing is not to walk alone, but to rely on each other as brothers and sisters, and especially under the leadership of the bishops, in a wise and realistic pastoral discernment.* [32]

Pope Francis is the first pope since Vatican II who has played no part in the work of the Council. He was a student in a Jesuit seminary at the time. There is no doubt that that he is very much a man of Vatican II

---

[31] VaticanII Declaration on Catholic Education, preface.
[32] Evangelii Gaudium.n. 33

which is frequently quoted in his Evangelii Gaudium. In one of his homilies as pope he said 'the Council was a beautiful work of the Holy Spirit. But after fifty years we have to ask have we done everything the Holy Spirit at the Council told us to do?' In his address to the Congregation for Catholic Education he spoke of how the celebration of the fiftieth anniversary of the *Declaration on Christian Education* ought to help us to reflect seriously and take on the responsibility 'to express the living presence of the Gospel in the field of education, of science and of culture'. And so he asks 'have we done everything the Holy Spirit in the Council has told to do?' Hence the publication of the document of the Congregation Educating Today and Tomorrow: A Renewing Passion with the principles, recommendations and guidelines which it sets out for discussion and action.

Vatican documents since the Council

For the fiftieth anniversary the Vatican Congregation has produced the working document on Catholic Education. It is intended to encourage discussion on the 'immense challenges' that face Catholic education world-wide. At the end of the document there was a questionnaire intended to encourage those with responsibilities in education and those with a special interest in it to reflect seriously on challenges which are highlighted and to discuss them in order to provide indications, suggestions and proposals for consideration at the international convention planned for 18-21 November 2015 in Rome.

This present text is intended to do something similar for those who may not have taken part in those initial discussions but who are involved in our schools and parishes to enable them to reflect on what is being done and on what we can do better in our Catholic schools. In the years since the Council the Congregation for Catholic Education - which is in fact the post-conciliar commission - has produced a number of significant documents and other papers on different aspects of education which underline the challenges and opportunities which have occurred in the past fifty years and which have encouraged discussion and led to the necessary action being taken to improve the Catholic life of the schools. These documents have proved invaluable in in-service days in schools [33] and have inspired teachers and all staff to reflect on and clarify their mission in times of rapid change.

I find that the text of this latest working document of the Congregation downloaded from the internet to be useful in highlighting 'the immense challenges' which educators in Catholic schools have to face and the opportunities that have arisen since the since the Declaration in 1965. A lot has changed in fifty years.

> Since the Council the historical and social context has changed remarkably both in terms of the world vision as well as ethical and political concepts. The 1960s were a time of confident expectations ...Compared to that time the scenario has deeply changed. The drive towards

[33] A number of these are discussed in my book *Serving the Young: Our Catholic Schools Today;* see titles and dates in appendix

secularisation has become more apparent. The increasingly faster globalisation process rather than favouring the promotion of individual freedom and greater integration between peoples, seems to limit individual freedom and exacerbate conflicts between different ways of looking at personal and collective life...

However, all the changes that have taken place since the 1960s not only have not weakened the teachings provided by the Council on educational issues, but have actually enhanced their prophetic scope. [34]

This change has been discussed in several Vatican documents, for example the quotation from The Catholic School in 1977 already cited: 'This is a time when Christianity demands to be clothed in new garments; when all manner of changes have been introduced in the Church and in secular life, and particularly, when a pluralist mentality dominates and the Christian Gospel is increasingly pushed to the side-lines'. Such is the Church and the world we now live in which is different in many ways from the Church and world of 1965.

The Vatican II Declaration on Christian Education

First of all let us look again at the *Declaration on Christian Education* approved by the Council Fathers on 28th October 1965. It is a rather brief document. It was

---

[34] Educating Today and Tomorrow p.4

'never centre stage at the Council'. In discussions before the final approval there was considerable dissatisfaction with the text because it was too wide spread and wide-ranging. Education was understood differently in different cultures and the situations of Catholic schools in those cultures varied considerably. Some at the Council wanted more said to meet the great variety of situations in different countries.

> For all the criticism the declaration received, it set out important principles and, in its approach and style, was congruent with the other documents of the council. As it was put to the vote, the commission made clear that, despite various stratagems floating in the assembly to revise it further, this was the final text. At the same time the commission emphasised, the document did not pretend to be the last word on the subject; indeed it provided direction to episcopal conferences and other bodies as they sought to adapt it to their circumstances. [35]

I shall now attempt a brief overview of some of the main principles raised in the Vatican II Declaration. It states that people are now more conscious of their own dignity and responsibility and are, therefore, keen to take an increasingly active role in social life and especially in the economic and political spheres. Accordingly, efforts are being made everywhere to ensure a continuing development of education. It is stressed that all people of whatever race, gender or age have, in virtue of their

---

[35] W. O'Malley, What Happened at Vatican II, Harvard University Press, 2008, p. 270

dignity as human persons, an inalienable right to education.

> True education aims to give people a formation which is directed towards their final goal and the good of that society to which they belong and in which, as adults, they will have their share of duties to perform.

Children and young people should be helped to develop harmoniously their physical, moral and intellectual qualities. They should be open to dialogue with others and should willingly devote themselves to the promotion of the common good.(n.1). All who are baptised have a right to Christian education which will gradually introduce them to the knowledge of the mystery of salvation and a greater appreciation of the gift of faith. They should learn to give witness to the hope that is in them and to promote the Christian concept of the world. Pastors are reminded of their grave obligation 'to do all in their power to ensure that this Christian education is enjoyed by all the faithful and especially the young who are the hope of the Church.' (n.2)

Great stress is put on the place and primary role of parents in the education of their children. In the family children will have their first experience of a well-balanced human society and of the Church. Education requires the help of society. The Church will offer its assistance for the good of society in this world and for the development of a world worthy of humanity.(n.3). Special importance is given to 'catechetical instruction' which illumines and strengthens the faith and to the 'media of social communication' (n.4). School is seen as of outstanding importance: it fosters a sense of values and prepares pupils for professional life. It provides for friendly contacts between pupils of different characters and backgrounds. Teachers have the important role of helping parents in carrying out their duties and such 'a vocation requires special qualities of mind and heart, most careful preparation and constant readiness to accept new ideas and to adapt the old' (n.5).

The support of the state is vital in safeguarding the rights and health of all. It must take seriously its duty of providing suitable teacher training and encourage associations of parents (n.6). The provision of sound moral and religious education is stressed. Priests and lay people are encouraged to teach Christian doctrine and to provide spiritual support. Again parents are reminded of their grave obligation in this regard. Help should be given to those who are taught in non-Catholic schools (n.7). Catholic schools should be zealous in the promotion of culture and the human formation of the young. It is seen as a special function of the Catholic school to develop in the school a community atmosphere 'animated by a spirit of freedom and love based on the Gospel'. The Catholic school, open as it should be, to modern developments prepares its pupils to contribute effectively to the welfare of humanity and to the work of the extension of the Kingdom of God. It can promote dialogue between the Church and the community at large. The teachers are reminded that it depends chiefly on them whether the Catholic school achieves its purpose and that they should be properly qualified and have adequate learning both religious and secular. They are also reminded of the great service they offer 'which is admirably suited to our time and indeed is very necessary' (n.8).

Considerable importance should be given to the establishment of different types of schools: professional and technical, institutes for adults, for the disabled and training colleges for teachers of religion. Pastors of the Church are exhorted 'to spare no sacrifice in caring for the poor, for those who are without family ties and for non-believers'. In establishing and conducting Catholic schools one must keep in mind modern developments. (n.9). Attention is then given to higher education, to colleges and universities. The setting up of theological faculties is recommended and entry to them 'should be made easy for students of great promise but of moderate resources, and especially for those from newly developed countries'. Spiritual care for students is stressed (n.10 & 11). Cooperation is to be encouraged at diocesan, national and international levels (n.12) Finally it affirms 'deep gratitude to all, priests, men and women religious, and laity who have devoted themselves to the all-important work of education and schools of all kinds and grades' (n.13)

Such is a brief overview of the some of the main principles covered in the declaration. Clearly, as is stated in the declaration, these principles call for further development and require adaptation to the different local situations of Catholic schools. In the years following the Council the Congregation for Catholic Education was established for this purpose. The documents which it published spell out a theological and spiritual vision which emphasise, as the document says, the 'need for Christian education to grow at the same time as human education, albeit respecting its Christian character, to prevent a situation in which the life of faith is experienced or perceived as being separate from other activities in human life.' [36]

The Vatican II Declaration fifty years on

On looking back over the last fifty years there is much to celebrate and be grateful for, while at the same time we must face the very real challenges with courage and determination to ensure we are faithful to the mission of the Church and the Catholic school in today's fast changing society. The working document states that this anniversary year 2015 is a suitable occasion 'for taking on board the recommendations of the Magisterium and sketching out guidelines for coming decades'. It sets out first of all some essential features of the Catholic school and then goes on to examine a number of current and future educational challenges. In the remainder of this chapter I shall concentrate on some of the recommendations and guidelines and shall consider how far we are succeeding in achieving some success in this regard. The challenges I shall consider in the following chapters.

The document asks 'what should schools be like?'

> Schools and universities are places where people learn to live their lives, achieve cultural growth, receive vocational training and engage in the

---
[36] *Educating Today and Tomorrow* p 5.

49

pursuit of the common good; they provide the occasion and opportunity to understand the present time and imagine the future of society and mankind. At the root of Catholic education is our Christian spiritual heritage, which is part of a constant dialogue with the cultural heritage and the conquests of science; Catholic schools and universities are educational communities where learning thrives on the integration between research, thinking and life experience. [37]

Again there is frequent mention of a dialogical approach as an essential aspect of Catholic education: it should be open to working with others and for the promotion of the common good. Catholic schools must collaborate with others who are part of our cultural heritage and those who are engaged in the serious development of science and of new scientific discoveries.

Schools and universities are places where students are introduced to knowledge and scientific research. One of teachers' main responsibilities is to attract younger generations towards knowledge and understanding its achievements and applications. Knowledge and research cannot be separated from a sense of ethics and transcendence: no real science can disregard ethical consequences and no real science drives us away from transcendence. Science and ethics, science and transcendence are not mutually

---

[37] op. cit. p. 6

exclusive, but come together for a greater and better understanding of man and the world. [38]

While this quotation may seem to apply especially to those teaching science to university students and sixth formers, it has implication for the way we approach the teaching of the scientific subjects and other subjects to whatever age in our schools: 'teachers must know how to present the essential elements of cultural heritage that has accumulated over time and how to present them to students'.

Some quality marks of the Catholic school

The document goes on to emphasise again that the aim of Catholic schooling is the integral education of the whole person and speaks of the central importance of a living context or climate of schools and universities. Catholic schools and universities educate people, first and foremost, through the living context i.e. the climate that both students and teachers establish in the environment where the teaching and learning activities take place. The climate or ethos is pervaded by the values that are being expressed and taught but also by the values that are lived out, by the quality of interpersonal relations between teachers and students and students amongst each other, by the care teachers devote to students and the local community needs, by the living testimony provided by teachers and the entire staff. [39]

---

[38] op. cit. p.7

[39] op. cit. p.6.

The document enumerates a number of the quality, distinctive marks of the Catholic school: respect for individual dignity; the wealth of opportunities offered to young people for them to grow and develop their abilities and talents; a balanced focus on the cognitive, affective, social, professional, ethical and spiritual aspects; encouragement for every pupil to develop in a climate of cooperation and solidarity; promotion of study and research with a great openness of mind and heart; respect for ideas, openness to dialogue, and the ability to interact and work together in a spirit of freedom and care. [40]

> Teaching that only promotes repetitive learning, without favouring students' active participation or sparking their curiosity, is not sufficiently challenging to elicit motivation. Learning through research and problem solving develops different and more significant cognitive and mental abilities, whereby students do more than just receiving information, while also stimulating teamwork. [41]

Teaching and learning does not only involve learning about the subject matter but must 'be nourished by mutual esteem, trust, respect and friendliness' between teachers and students. When learning takes place 'in a context where the subjects who are involved feel a sense of belonging, it is quite different from a situation in which learning occurs in a climate of individualism, antagonism and mutual coldness'.[42] Again great emphasis is placed

---

[40] op. cit. p. 7

[41] op. cit. P.7

on creating a sense of community within the school, of healthy relationships and enabling students to feel they belong rather than creating an atmosphere that is negative and unfriendly. Since the Vatican Council there has been 'an important advance in the way the Catholic school is thought of: the transition from the school as an institution to the school as community.'[43] This should be a distinctive feature of our schools.

While schools provide students with training that will enable them to enter the labour market and social life with adequate skills, it is not enough.

> Learning can also provide the opportunity to open students' hearts and minds to the mystery and wonder of the world and nature, to self-consciousness and awareness, to responsibility towards creation, to the Creator's immensity' [44].

Such learning which opens hearts and minds to 'mystery and wonder' is possible within every subject of the curriculum - Religious Education, English, Geography, History, the Sciences, Music, Drama, etc. There can and should be more interdisciplinary learning with each subject not being seen as an end in itself, cut off from other forms of learning. Nor is the school a complete learning environment if what they have learnt does not also become an occasion to serve the community. Teachers should provide their students 'opportunities to

---

[42] op. cit. p. 74

[43] Lay Catholics in Schools n.31.

[44] Educating Today and Tomorrow. p.8

realise the social impact of what they are studying, thus favouring the discovery of the link between school and life, as well as the development of a sense of responsibility and active citizenship' [45]. The role of School Councils which meet and discuss then suggest to the some of the Leadership Team possible improvements to the school environment and the general wellbeing of students has much to be encouraged and should be respected by the staff in the school. It develops in the students' real responsibility for their fellow students and prepares them to take up responsibilities in their communities and beyond. Such aspects were very much to the forefront of Pope Francis' talks to teachers and students.

There is much to celebrate

In my experience, and I am sure in the experience of many teachers, many of these recommendations and guidelines are being acted on and schools have much to celebrate as they strive to achieve what it means to be a Catholic school in today's society. Most schools have a clear mission statement based on the person of Jesus the Christ and the values He preached and lived; this is often posted in various places throughout the school as a reminder to students, staff and visitors of the Catholic mission of the school. It is often brought up in assemblies and in briefing meetings for members of staff. Often the school's mission statement takes and adapts John Paul IIs statement.

---

[45] op. cit. p. 8

The Catholic school is for the human person and of human persons. The person of each individual human being, in his or her material and spiritual needs, is the heart of the Church's teaching: this is why the promotion of the human person is the goal of the Catholic school. [46]

At the very heart of the educational mission of the Catholic school is the belief in the God-given dignity of each and every person and in the significance, value and worth of all human life. One of my favourite quotations from the Vatican documents on education is one from The Catholic School where it states that the school's energy derives from Christ: 'it thus creates in the school community an atmosphere permeated with the Gospel spirit of freedom and love. In this setting pupils will experience their dignity as persons before they know its definition' [47].

Nowadays on the whole schools are happier, more welcoming and supportive of students and parents and of practical service to the local and wider community. There is good academic achievement, and outstanding pastoral care which supports the needs of each student in their own development; Catholic schools are remarkably successful with students from poor and deprived localities; they have special care for the academically, physically or emotionally disadvantaged. Our schools are not exclusive: currently 29.8% of pupils in Catholic schools and colleges are of other denominations and

---

[46] Quoted in *The Catholic School on the Threshold of the Third Millennium* n. 9
[47] *The Catholic School* n.55

faiths or none; the figure in Wales is 42% of pupils. They are popular with parents and in places there is an increasing demand for places. Catholic schools have a greater proportion of pupils from ethnic minority backgrounds. [48]

There is greater appreciation of the need to teach not only the Catholic religion, though it is central and given priority, but to help students understand and respect the other major religions and faiths, and be open to cultural and religious dialogue in accordance with their age, abilities and situation. There is a vast amount of fund raising for good causes and being aware of the underlying reasons why this is necessary and very human and Christian. Many sixth formers help out in various projects for example the HCPT pilgrimages to Lourdes. The older students attend to the needs of the disabled and organise and attend the religious activities as well as the fun and games which keep them fully participating in the entertainment. The students speak of how much they gain from the experiences. There are also projects for those in greater need when a number of sixth formers volunteer to spend time in the so called developing countries during the summer holidays teaching and caring for those who are less fortunate. Many lasting friendships and communications often spring from these experiences and some take up the vocation of volunteering later and during a gap year. In some schools and colleges half or more of sixth formers follow R.E. courses engaging in theological and philosophical discussion and debate.

---

[48] *Catholic Education in England and Wales*, Catholic Education Service 2014

No call for complacency

We cannot guarantee that all Catholic schools strive to or do fulfil this mission equally well. Each school will have its own successes. They should be thanked and praised for what they do. The pope himself is well aware that teachers are not appreciated as much as they should be as we shall see later. There is much to celebrate and congratulate good schools for. However, we must not be complacent or too full of self-congratulations. In each school or college, staff and students, Governors and parents, must be constantly prepared to ensure that they strive to live out its mission and to fulfil the expectations and challenges given us by the Council and Pope Francis. He reminds us, as is cited in the second of the opening quotations of this chapter, we should not walk alone but in union with many others, especially the bishops, we should undertake with them 'a realistic, pastoral discernment'. In this time of recession and financial cutbacks dioceses need to continue a vibrant service of support for the mission of our schools. The success of our schools should be a major concern for all in the Church: Bishops, Diocesan Advisers, Head Teachers, staff and all involved in our schools, they need our support and appreciation.

In its conclusion the document speaks of school as a learning community as well as a place of teaching and of the need for collaboration of all involved in the school.

> Teaching is not only a process through which knowledge or training are provided, but also

guidance for everyone to discover their talents, develop professional skills and take important intellectual, social and political responsibilities in local communities. Even more than this, teaching means to accompany young people in their search for truth and beauty, for what is right and good. The effectiveness of collective action, involving both teaching and administrative staff, is given by shared values and the fact of being a learning community, in addition to teaching. You are all educators there is no delegates in this field. Thus collaboration in spirit of unity and community among the various educators is essential and must be fostered and encouraged.[49]

The central role of teachers and others is constantly appreciated and acknowledged. They must never be in doubt about the fact that they constitute an element of great hope for the Church and for society. The Church puts its trust in them entrusting them with the task of gradually bringing about an integration of temporal reality with the Gospel so that the Gospel can reach into the lives of all men and women.[50] This is our mission and in explaining it and reflecting on it with staff in briefings or in-service days we must ensure that all feel they have an active and positive part to play without in any way letting them feel excluded. We all have a part in achieving this mission which should be appreciated by all, especially the head and senior leadership team.

---

[49] Educating Today and Tomorrow. p. 20

[50] *Lay Catholics in School* n.81.

The school must be a community whose values are communicated through the interpersonal and sincere relationships of its members and through both individual and corporate adherence to the outlook of life that permeates the school. [51]

---

[51] *The Catholic School*.3

PAUSE FOR REFLECTION

In the last 50 years much has changed in society and the Church. What would you say are the main changes that impact on what we seek to do in our schools both positively and negatively?

Is your school constantly working to ensure that the 'quality marks' enumerated in the document are part of the lived experience of students and staff? Which are most evident? Which need attention?

Great stress is put on the community, family atmosphere which should be found in Catholic schools. Do staff and students experience this in your school? Can you say in what ways?

Which good aspects of Catholic education outlined in the document would you consider worthy of celebration and congratulations in your school? How and when do the staff and Governors celebrate these with students and parents?

Chapter Four

CURRENT TENSIONS AND CHALLENGES

> *Finally, this document is also addressed to Christian communities, so that they may reflect on the importance of Catholic education in the context of New Evangelisation. The text can be used to effect a pastoral evaluation of this area of the Church's apostolate; it can also be used it promote various activities for updating and forming those who work in Catholic schools and universities.* [52]
>
> *If we look at the great educational challenges that we will face soon, we must keep the memory of God made flesh in the history of mankind – in our history – alive.* [53]

In the last chapter we considered some of the main recommendations and guidelines set out in the document Educating today and Tomorrow: A Renewing Passion and looked at how in our schools in Britain we have tried to act upon these and how we can claim some success by examining the data and facts available. The document then goes on to outline some of the significant tensions and challenges which we are with us today and will be with us in the future and to which we are called upon to

---

[52] Educating Today and Tomorrow, Presentation

[53] op. cit. p.9

respond. I now give attention to those which seem more relevant to our situation.

The challenge of diversity of arising from different needs of students

Teachers are called upon to face the many tensions and challenges which the recognition and respect for psychological, social, cultural and religious diversity give rise to. Teachers must be open to and professionally knowledgeable about the differences in needs of students the gifted, those with special needs and the others with a variety of different needs. They should recognise and appreciate this diversity and attend to the needs of all and ensure that members of staff can give adequate attention to each student.

> Teachers are called upon to rise up to a major educational challenge, which is the recognition, respect and enhancement of diversity. Psychological, social, cultural and religious diversity should not be denied, but rather considered as an opportunity and a gift...Teachers must be open and professionally knowledgeable when they are leading classes where diversity is recognised, accepted and appreciated as an educational asset that is beneficial to everyone. Those who find themselves in greater difficulties, who are poorer, more fragile or needy, should not be seen as a burden or obstacle but should be at the centre of the school's attention and concern. [54]

---

[54] op. cit. p.8

In the desire to achieve well in the ratings of the league tables special care must be given to 'the more fragile and needy', they must not be overlooked or seen as 'a burden or obstacle' holding the school back from achieving the targets. The kind of education that is promoted by Catholic schools 'is not aimed at establishing an elitist meritocracy'. The pursuit of quality and excellence is indeed important. However this must not be achieved by ignoring or neglecting the needs - psychological, emotional, academic and social of individual students.

> We should never forget that students have very specific needs, are often going through difficulties and deserve a pedagogical attention that takes their needs into account...An increasing number of students have been wounded during their childhood. Poor school performance is increasing and requires a preventive kind of education, as well as specific training for teachers. [55]

The Vatican document acknowledges that it is not easy for schools to be 'inclusive', open to this diversity and able to help those who are experiencing difficulties of different kinds. This recalls the description of the types of students in our schools outlined in the 1997 Vatican Document, 'The Catholic School on the Threshold of the Third Millennium', cited at the end of the first chapter.

> Young people can be found again among those who have lost all sense of the meaning of life and lack any type of inspiring ideal, those to whom no values are proposed and who do not know the

---

[55] op. cit. p.12

beauty of faith, who come from families which are broken and incapable of love, often living in situations of material and spiritual poverty...To these new poor the Catholic school turns in a spirit of love.

Supporting Learning Centres which cater for all these needs and provide 'a preventive kind of education' supported with a highly qualified staff with time and the necessary resources should be a strong feature of all Catholic schools. Many schools are quite outstanding in their pastoral care in this regard but we should always be open to improvement in this regard.

Challenges arising from the diversity of cultural and social situations of schools

There is another very real diversity which is often overlooked when talking of Catholic schools and that is the social, cultural and religious diversity which exists in the location and cultural situation of many of our schools, often in the same diocese. When we talk of the Catholic school, there is the danger that we talk of an ideal or in abstract, of a school that is without real pupils and staff and which is not situated in a particular locality. When we consider the educational pastoral service which each school should provide we have to bear in mind such factors as the economic, social, cultural, ethnic, racial, religious and family situations which impinge on the situation and context in which the school seeks to serve the children, young people, their families and the local community.

Some years ago I touched on this aspect when addressing the Deputy Heads of primary schools in a large diocese. At one point I asked them to turn to the people sitting near them and say something about the particular situation and location of their own school upon how these factors might impinge on what they tried to do. I then asked a group of three to share with the whole group. One described a pleasant leafy suburb with a large number of professional people, mostly white, with a fairly large percentage of practising and committed Catholics and a flourishing parish life. The second served an urban locality, in a culturally mixed area. The pupils came from a variety of cultures, for many English was a second language. Many were Catholic, with a growing number of other faiths applying for places. There was considerable unemployment and poverty. The third served an area partly urban, partly rural, with pupils of different social backgrounds with many non-practising families or families who occasionally attended the parish; there were a good number of broken homes in the care of single parents and a good number of pupils who were not Catholic. These are some features of the diversity of situations in which our schools seek to fulfil their mission of serving the young, their families and the locality: 'Catholic schools and universities fulfil their task, which is mission and service, in very different cultural and social contexts'. [56]

The documents of the Congregation for Catholic Education and documents from our Bishops' Conference and The Catholic Education Service are very much aware

---

[56] Educating Today and Tomorrow p.8

of this diversity and of the fact that schools are increasingly finding themselves in the second and third situations of those described above. Pope Francis frequently speaks of this challenge facing Catholic schools in addressing the needs of parents, students and teachers in to-day's multi-cultural, multi-ethnic, multi-religious society and in a society indifferent to religion. He is strong in defending full respect for each one's dignity. He speaks frequently of the pastoral care of the poor and those who are different in their practice and commitment to the Catholic faith tradition. In one of his talk to the teachers in Buenos Aires he posed the very challenging question: 'Do we believe in our pupils, in the families of our neighbourhood, in our people?[57] For him this is an important aspect of teaching and one we shall return to again. He maintains that teachers need preparation and support in this new and demanding mission of the Catholic school. This calls for discussion and respectful dialogue between schools and parishes in the context of new evangelisation to find realistic ways they can work together and share resources without over burdening already busy teachers. More will be said on this towards the end of the chapter when considering support for families and carers.

---

[57] Education for Choosing Life p.35

The challenges of religious formation in our pluralist society

A clear challenge today is the decline in practice of and commitment to the Christian faith particularly in Europe. As the document puts it we are left with the questions:

> How are we going to educate them to faith and in faith? How will we establish the preliminary conditions to accept this gift, to educate them to gratitude, to a sense of awe, to asking themselves questions, to develop a sense of justice and consistency? How will we educate them to prayer? [58]

These are indeed questions that are constantly asked about younger pupils in our Catholic primary schools and older students in secondary schools. There are no quick easy answers. The latest Vatican document, as have many previous documents, acknowledges that 'a growing number of young people are drifting away from the institutional Church. Religious ignorance and illiteracy are rising. Catholic education is an unglamorous mission'. Teachers often feel the burden of this 'unglamorous mission' especially when they receive unfavourable reports from inspectors or parents who unfairly criticise aspects of the school and when some Catholics too readily accuse the school of failing of passing on the faith with little true understanding of the difficulties they face or any real appreciation of what they achieve. This gives rise to the question 'who are Catholic schools for?' Catholics give different answers but in the

---

[58] op. cit. p.10

perspective of Jesus and of Pope Francis the answer must surely be 'for all, the weak and the strong'.

> Christians have the duty to proclaim the Gospel without excluding anyone. Instead of seeking to impose new obligations, they should appear as people who wish to share their joy, who point to a horizon of beauty and who invite others to a delicious banquet. It is not by proselytising that the Church grows, but 'by attraction' [59]

This feature of Catholic schools has been put rather well in a 1981 report to the bishops more than thirty years ago and still rings true today.

> One of the paradoxical strengths of the Church is that it is in every sense Catholic, it is for the weak and the strong, for those who fail as well as for those who succeed, for sinners as well as for saints. It could be the ability of our schools to be Catholic in that sense, that could have something unique to contribute to education in our country as well as their being a sign of living and urgent faith. [60]

This is 'new evangelisation': meeting people where they are at, while appealing to them and sharing joy with them, inviting them by 'attraction' rather than by new 'obligations' and strict demands. This calls for greater understanding and collaboration between schools and the priests and people in the parishes.

---

[59] *Evangelii Gaudium* n.15

[60] *Signposts and Homecomings* p.5

Teaching R. E. in Catholic schools in today's culture

One of the most important challenges will be

to foster a greater cultural openness amongst cultures and between different religions, there cannot be any real dialogue if educators themselves have not been formed and helped to deepen their faith and personal beliefs.' [61]'

This makes demands on teachers and on all who have responsibility for their training and formation in today's society and cultural context. Religious Education is being overlooked as a serious subject of the curriculum in many places. In schools in England and Wales it is no longer recognised by the Government as a core subject for GCSE. However, in Catholic schools it is still given that status and importance. Recent discussions among those involved in curriculum are insisting that two religions be studied at GCSE. Our bishops have no problem with that as long as the Catholic religion is one of the two religions studied. The serious study of a second religion can only help create greater mutual understanding and social coherence. R.E. departments, advised by diocesan advisers, will decide on the second religion to be studied in the light of the situation they find themselves in. There is much to be said for a study of the Jewish faith and way of life since it is the root of our Christian faith. In certain places where there is a large Muslim community it would seem only right to

---

[61] Educating Today and Tomorrow pp.13 – 15.

study Islam in some depth which will also benefit community living and greater social cohesion. This would seem advisable in the light of the unease after the Paris and other incidents. In different situations there may be value in the study of other belief traditions such as that of Sikhism or Buddhism. In Key Stages 1 and 2 in the primary school and in Key Stage 3 in the secondary school aspects of these religions will be studied in ways suited to the age and capabilities of the pupils. For A level Religious Studies in Catholic schools there have been discussions with the Catholic Education Service, the National Board representing the dioceses, as well as departments of theology in Catholic universities. This augurs well for improved academically sound and appealing courses.

Knowledge of students' real needs

The document states that 'religion courses require an in-depth knowledge of young people's real needs, because this will provide the foundation on which a personal faith can be built'.

> Teachers, school Heads, administrative the whole professional staff is called upon to present faith as an attractive option: with a humble, a supportive attitude. The model is provided by Jesus Christ and his disciples in Emmaus: we must start from young people's life experience but also from that of co-workers, to provide an unconditional service. Actually, educating young people to serve and give

themselves freely is one of the hallmarks of Catholic schools, in the past as well as the future. [62]

We are reminded that we should present the Christian faith 'as an attractive option', not as yet another obligation. We cannot do this successfully without 'an in-depth knowledge of young people's real needs'. The model of Jesus with the two disciples on the road to Emmaus is presented to us as a sensitive way of educating to and in faith. Jesus accompanies the two, asks them 'what is the matter, what is troubling them?' and listens to their story. He does not rush in with ready-made answers and gradually opens up the passages of scripture which they failed to understand concerning himself and his death and resurrection. He has 'a humble, a supportive attitude'. In the final chapter of the book Soil for the Seed I reflect on this Gospel story from two angles: firstly, Jesus as the model evangelist with the two downcast disciples and secondly, the two disciples as examples of those frustrated and discouraged in the mission of educating and evangelising. [63]

Religious education aims to give knowledge; it is distinct from catechesis

The documents clearly say that any distinction between 'knowing and believing must be respected'[64]. This distinction is discussed in a number of Vatican

---

[62] *Educating Today and Tomorrow* p.II

[63] Soil for the Seed, J. Gallagher, McCrimmons, Great Wakering p.309 -322

[64] Statement on Religious Education, Catholic Bishops' Conference, England and Wales, 2000.

documents including the one on educating to intercultural dialogue.

> Moreover, it must be pointed out that teaching the Catholic religion in schools has its own aims, different from those of catechesis. In fact, while catechesis promotes personal adherence to Christ and maturing of Christian life, school teaching gives the students knowledge about Christianity's identity and Christian life. [65].

This has been a cause of tension and difference of opinion especially when considering new R.E. texts published since Vatican II for primary and secondary schools. Bishops' Conferences are reminded of their grave duty of providing such courses which include 'knowledge and critical learning concerning all religions in society'. In several Church documents we are asked to ensure that R.E. entails 'learning about' and 'learning from' religious beliefs, rituals and practices. It is not sufficient to know about these, but to explore why these are important and significant to believers, Christians and others. The outcome of Catholic religious education 'Is religiously literate young people who have the knowledge, understanding and skills, appropriate to their age and capacity, to think spiritually, ethically and theologically, and who are aware of the demands of religious commitment in everyday life' [66].

---

[65] Educating to Intercultural Dialogue in Catholic schools: Living in Harmony for a Civilisation of Love n. 74;

[66] Curriculum Directory p. 10

In their Statement on Religious Education in Catholic Schools in the year 2000 the bishops of England and Wales state that

> Classroom R.E. will be a challenging educational engagement between the pupil, the teacher and the authentic subject material. This will be done in the context of a lived Christian faith which inspires and challenges all our educational activities in the school.
>
> R.E. teaching in a Catholic School will be enlightened by the faith of the school community and by the faith of the R.E. teacher. Its educational focus will be formed and enhanced by the vitality of faith...When classroom R.E. displays this educational characteristic, then its specific contribution to the life of the Catholic school, which as a whole is a catechetical community, becomes apparent' [67].

The ethos and all our educational activities, the whole life of the school, should be a lived experience inspired and challenged by our Catholic faith and is the responsibility of all who are involved in the daily life of the school; it is not the sole responsibility of the religious education department, the chaplain or the senior leadership. This at the same time should always be coupled with great respect for the conscience and freedom of each individual.

---

[67] Statement on Religious Education in Catholic Schools – issued by the Bishops' Conference of England and Wales, 2000; see J. Gallagher, Soil for the Seed p. 292.

The importance of the study of other faiths in Catholic Schools

With regard to the teaching of other religions the bishops have issued guidelines in various documents and clearly state that 'we view our Catholic schools as part of our mission not only in relation to the Catholic population but also in regard to how Catholics relate to people of other religions'.[68]. They speak of dialogue as 'not so much an idea to be studied as a way of living in positive relationships with others'.

> Interreligious dialogue, then, as the Catholic Church understands it, includes simply living as good neighbours with those of other religions, or working together in matters of common concern, such as in issues of justice, peace, the integrity of creation and so forth. It includes a willingness, according to circumstances, to try to understand better the religion of one's neighbours, and to experience something of their religious life and culture. In other words, dialogue is above all a frame of mind, an attitude.[69].

Within our schools 'we are seeking to educate all pupils of whatever religion to be able to live a life that integrates their beliefs with all other aspects of what it means to be human'. In order to do so students must learn to live alongside others who are different and hold alternative views, including religious views.[70] The Catholic Education

---

[68] Meeting God in Friend and Stanger: Fostering respect and mutual understanding between the religions, 2010, n.196

[69] op. cit. n. 3

Services' 2008 document speaks of three distinct areas of dialogue which have a place in our schools: the dialogue of life (living together in harmony), the dialogue of action (working together for common causes), the dialogue of theological exchange (studying the tenets and practice of other religions – learning about and learning from).[71]

> The vast majority of Catholics will never enter into interreligious dialogue in a formal academic sense but each and every Christian or person of another religion is called to enter into interreligious dialogue by virtue of the fact that we live in a world of many religions...Catholic schools can help us prepare for that lifetime of interreligious dialogue.[72].

Are our religious education texts of sufficient standard to enable teachers to educate pupils in understanding and appreciation of the Catholic faith tradition and that of other religious faiths? The recent resource Come and See for the primary years, under the auspices of the National Project and the work of a number of diocesan advisers, is of a high standard and quality in this regard. Work is beginning by diocesan advisers and R.E. teachers in updating resources for key stage 3: The People of God – Called to Serve which also is of a very high standard and quality. Both are published as productions of the National Project. However, we have to ask ourselves the

---

[70] op. cit. n. 201

[71] Catholic Schools, Children of Other Faiths and Social Cohesion, Cherishing Education for Human Growth, CES

[72] Meeting God in Friend and Stanger n. 207

serious question 'Are teachers confident enough to teach this adequately?' This is a tension felt by many, especially R.E. Co-ordinators in primary schools, and a very real challenge for all teachers of R.E. in secondary Catholic schools. More serious help from diocesan advisers and collaboration between schools will be needed.

The challenge of living values which should permeate the life of the school

The document again reminds us that

> School communities that are inspired by the values of the Catholic faith transpose their vision of the person – which is a hallmark of humanistic-Christian tradition – into the way the school is organised and into what is taught not in order to oppose other cultures and religious faiths, but to engage in dialogue with them.[73].

This is a delicate task which seeks to avoid relativism, on the one hand, and a dogmatic fundamentalism on the other. I discuss some of these concerns in Serving the Young: Our Catholic Schools Today' [74] In that text I refer to a number of the documents of the Congregation for Catholic Education which 'do not provide a quick answer to contemporary problems, but give a direction which can

---

[73] Educating Today and Tomorrow.8

[74] See also my book *Soil for the Seed: Historical, Pastoral and Theological Reflections on Educating to and in the Faith*, Mc Crimmons 2001, especially chapters 14 & 15.

begin to solve them' [75]. Some of the ways we can seek to educate the young in the faith are outlined by Pope Benedict in his various addresses on this theme during his visit to Britain. We have to bear in mind what Pope Francis says and his call for a new language and a pastoral ministry in a missionary approach which is much more suited to the needs and searching of young people in our multi-cultural, multi-faith and secular society. Much can be learnt from the approach of Don Bosco in his mission of educating and evangelising the young. We have to ask ourselves whether we are providing sufficient training and support for all our teachers, especially R.E. teachers, for primary and secondary schools.

The challenge of the media

We are challenged by the fact that 'learning does not take place exclusively within school'. Our current cultural context 'is strongly characterised by the pervasiveness of the new technological languages and new opportunities for informal learning'. Schools are no longer the only learning environment and they 'have lost their traditional educational primacy...schools have to deal with scenarios where information is more broadly available, in massive uncontrollable amounts'. The young use the internet, Facebook and Twitter, to name only a few of the technological tools available, and they are well versed in their use, often uncritical or unaware of the dangers.

---

[75] *The Catholic School* n. 67

'Learning opportunities outside school are increasingly widespread and impactful'.

> Since schools are no longer the only learning environment for young people, and not even the most important one, and virtual communities are acquiring a remarkable importance, schooling must face a new challenge: that is, helping students develop the necessary critical tools to avoid being dominated by the power of new media.[76]

Teachers in schools and parents will be well aware of the negative features of this new media but they must also be open to the positive aspects and to help students to use it well and critically.

The document goes on to acknowledge that easy access to information is readily available in the media and there is little critical awareness which results in widespread superficiality among students, parents and even teachers. This impoverishes reason, imagination and creative thinking. The number of teachers who are believers is also shrinking. This increasing indifference among many baptised Catholics and others, together with the increasing multiculturalism and multi-religiosity is a challenge for all who have educational responsibilities in our Catholic schools.

---

[76] Educating Today and Tomorrow p.12

The challenge of supporting families

Another challenging terrain for Catholic schools is relations with families, many of whom are going through a deep crisis and need support, solidarity, involvement and even formation.

> Teachers, parents and school heads - together with students – make up a broad educational community that is called upon to work together with Christian institutions...sensitive to individual needs and is able to systematically help poorer students and families...This is the approach Catholic schools should have towards young people, through dialogue, in order to present them with a view regarding the Other and others that is open, peaceful and enticing.[77]

This calls for serious thought. Recently in 2014 the Department for Evangelisation and Catechesis of the Bishops' Conference published 'A Case Study of Catholic Primary School Parents in England and Wales'. The research focused on the spiritual needs and interests, as well as the faith and practice, of Catholic parents of children of primary schools in England and Wales. While only looking at parents with primary school children the findings are of wider interest. The reasons why baptised Catholic parents choose a Catholic primary school when they do not actively participate in the Catholic Church are complex. The chief reasons for their choice 'were academic reputation; good values, location; the teaching of the Catholic faith; and the Catholic ethos'. The

---

[77] Educating Today and Tomorrow p. II

academic reputation was of paramount importance. Pastoral care was considered important. The teaching of the Catholic faith ranked highly and was seen 'to have a relaxed and 'fun' approach to the teaching, 'it was not forced upon the children'; a number of parents wanted the teaching of the Church to be in general terms, they wanted the child to make his/her own mind up about matters of faith. The participating in Mass in the school with the children was for many their only experience of a Catholic Mass. The majority of parents mentioned the presence of the parish priest in the school and this role was much appreciated by parents. With the decline in number of priests and clustering of parishes such a pastoral presence of the priest may not be as readily available in the very near future.

The need for greater dialogue between schools, parishes and dioceses

As I have said before, more discussions and dialogue between schools, parishes and dioceses about the appointment of pastoral workers or chaplains will be needed to face this issue in the light of new evangelisation. Some of the major projects to which we ought to give more serious thought will be how Catholic schools, parishes and homes may work more effectively together. They should not be overly caught up in their own distinct world with its own specific problems, perhaps being rather cynical and critical of the good being done in the others. It will be easier for primary schools to work more closely with parishes and families;

most are involved in sacramental preparation for Catholic pupils and some organise parenting courses. In this year when special emphasis is put on education in our schools in this fiftieth anniversary year of the Declaration on Christian Education and with stress on the needs and care of families which will be the concern of the coming Synod on the Family, it would seem the appropriate time for this to be given more serious thought. Secondary schools which serve Catholic students from a number of parishes will need to have to dialogue with parish councils on how together they may set up realistic and practical ways of achieving this common mission. The good working relationships between school, home and parish are vitally important for the holistic, integral education in the context of evangelisation which we seek to provide in our schools.

> Partnership between a Catholic school and the families of students must continue and be strengthened: not simply to deal with academic problems that may arise but rather so that the educational goals of the school can be achieved. Close cooperation with the family is especially important when treating sensitive issues such as religious, moral, or sexual education, orientation towards a profession, or a choice of one's vocation in life. It is not a question of convenience, but a partnership based on faith. Catholic tradition teaches that God has bestowed on the family its own specific educational mission.[78]

---

[78] The Religious Dimension of Education in a Catholic School n.42

PAUSE FOR REFLECTION

How does your school meet the diversity of needs among students – the gifted and those with special needs? How qualified are teachers in these areas?

How does the cultural and social situation of the school influence what you try to do – positively and negatively - in the mission within the school and community?

How does your school prepare students to play an active part in today's multi-cultural, multi-religious and in world which is indifferent to religion? What are the potential and difficulties in trying to achieve this?

How does the school educate students to use the media critically but wisely?

What is being done to support families? What more could be done?

How could schools work more closely and efficiently with people in the parishes in the common mission of education and evangelisation?

Chapter Five

RECRUITING AND RETAINING QUALIFIED TEACHERS IN CATHOLIC SCHOOLS

Nowadays education is going through rapid changes. The generation which is addressed is changing quickly as well, therefore each educator must constantly face a situation which, as Pope Francis put it, 'provides us with new challenges which sometimes are difficult for us to understand.[79]

In this kind of cultural context, teacher training becomes essential and requires rigour and depth...This kind of training is urgent if we want to rely on teachers who are committed to and concerned with our Educational Project's evangelical identity and its implementation in the future. [80]

Pope Francis laid great emphasis on the training of teachers and all those involved in education in his address to the members of the Congregation for Catholic Education. We are all very much aware that we are in a constantly fast changing word where nothing seems to stand still for very long. We can be either bogged down in nostalgia for the way things used to be or acknowledge

---

[79] *Educating Today And Tomorrow p.10*

[80] op. cit. p. 15

the changes and courageously face the consequences. This does not mean that we simply ditch the past but rather, while seeking to preserve and develop what was of value in what went before, we seek to adapt to the new situations and make the necessary changes that the times and the needs and concerns of the people may call for. Karl Rahner once wrote: 'The new historic situation confronts the old task – old and ever new; out of the fusion of task and situation will emerge the new service to which we are committed'. Pope Francis in his discussions with the teachers of Buenos Aires put it this way: 'it is a matter of creating, of beginning to put in place the bricks of a new edifice in the middle of history, that is to say, located in a present that has a past and – let us hope – also a future.[81]' This task is often demanding and far from easy and has its risks. Yet we should remind ourselves that it is a constant feature in the history of the Church, of the struggles of Christians as they faced what each generation saw as a crisis in Christian beliefs and values or the way of life of the followers of Jesus. Right from the very beginning the Church faced such challenges.

> The very fact that Christians have four gospels and not one is a powerful symbol of how preaching the Good News was shaped from the beginning by needs of different audiences or cultures. That the New Testament is written and comes down to us in Greek, and not in the language of Jesus himself, is an indication of a dramatic and painful decision by

---

[81] Education for Choosing Life p.10

the early Church to reach out beyond the Jewish cities to the culture of the Gentiles. [82]

For the first Christians who were Palestinian Jews it took time and courage for them to gradually open themselves to the needs of those interested in Christianity who were of the Hellenistic culture - Hellenistic Jews and Hellenistic Gentiles. These early disciples spread as faithfully as they could the Good News of Jesus, but as they tried to explain it more clearly, especially to people of a different culture, they were forced – some willingly and others reluctantly – to express it in categories of thought and language more suited to the Greco-Roman mentality and culture. We can overlook just how such a step was for them a dramatic, painful and courageous decision.

I think we are in a somewhat similar situation today as we face our multi-ethnic, multi-cultural, multi-faith society, a society which is on the whole indifferent to religion and faith. In particular we are facing something of a similar crisis in our Catholic schools in today's cultural context in Britain. Education, teaching and schooling are inevitably caught up in these rapid cultural changes. These can mean for us as for the early Christians that we have to make dramatic and sometimes painful choices which we must face and carefully and responsibly undertake the necessary adaptations which may be called for. Britain is now a multi-ethnic, multi-cultural, multi-religious and a very secular society in

---

[82] M. P. Gallagher, *Clashing Symbols*, Darton Longman & Todd, 1997, p. 101

which faith and religion if acknowledged should remain private and have no voice in the public domain.

> This is a particularly important task for us, in that the social and cultural changes that we are seeing place before us the need of finding new forms of dialogue and coexistence in a pluralist society, through which differences come to be accepted and respected, and to strengthen the spaces and topics of meeting and concord. [83]

Different types of schools and pathways to teacher qualification.

We are now faced with the fact that there are many different types of Catholic schools: maintained, grammar, independent, academies, free schools, joint Anglican and Catholic schools, Catholic schools with a large percentage of pupils of other faiths, Sixth Form Colleges. Some of these developments have occurred in the past few years or so. Catholics express different and often strong views on these various types of schools, on the general education they provide and on how they uphold and develop their Catholic character and mission in today's society. There is some controversy and uncertainty about academies, free schools and those with a large number of students who are not Catholic. We need only read the Catholic papers to discover the strongly held and divided opinions of Catholics in this regard. The educational teams of different dioceses, under the guidance of the

---

[83] *Education for Choosing Life* p.110

bishop, have their own views and reasoned arguments for their decisions. If we adopt the pastoral and missionary style of Pope Francis we will seek to meet the needs of students and families in each situation while upholding the essential belief in the holistic approach central to our faith vision.

> While all Catholic schools should adhere to the basic principles and motivation for Catholic schooling, each will seek to fulfil its mission in this place and with these people. The Christian motivation for this can be found in our belief in and theology of the Incarnation. Jesus became one of us in a particular time and a particular place. The incarnation is the acceptance of the human condition with all its implications. [84]

There are now also a variety of pathways to qualify as a teacher: following courses in colleges or universities with practical experience in schools or a school-led training which provides hands-on teacher training supported by experienced teachers based in a particular school, with experience of teaching in a second school. These can have consequences for the way we seek to promote and develop the Catholic ethos or environment which we claim should form the distinctive features of our Catholic schools and colleges.

> Clearly there is a great debate bubbling up about the future of teacher education between Catholic academics, teachers, church leaders and

---

[84] J. Gallagher, Serving the Young: Our Catholic Schools Today, Don Bosco Publications, p.48.

politicians. The outcome could determine the future of Catholic teaching and the prospects for our Catholic universities for decades to come. The stakes could not be higher. [85]

These developments cause us to pause and seriously think about how best we may prepare teachers in our schools, especially new teachers with a varying commitment to the Christian faith and those who are of other faiths or no faith, to come to a respectful understanding of the values enshrined in the education we offer in our schools. It raises questions about how we enable them to play a full, conscious and active part in maintaining and developing our vision of integral education of the whole person while respecting their own convictions. It also raises questions about the human resources available in dioceses to enable this, such as the number and qualification of school advisers.

There are now fewer Catholic universities and colleges

Long gone are the days when teacher training for Catholic schools was done almost exclusively in Catholic colleges with practical training in Catholic schools and when we could readily assume that teacher training provided a basic or substantial appreciation of such values and ways of doing things in our schools. There are now only a few Catholic or Anglican-Catholic Colleges, ecumenical Colleges, which offer such training: St Mary's

---

[85] J. Sutcliffe, Teaching the Teacher, the Tablet, 5th February 2011.

University, Twickenham, Trinity University Leeds, Newman University Birmingham (Catholic), Roehampton University London and Hope University Liverpool (Ecumenical). There has been a great reduction in former Catholic and Anglican Teacher Training Colleges. However, there are a number of colleges and universities which offer a sound study of Catholic theology.

In an in-service day for Induction Tutors in our Catholic schools some years ago I discovered that the majority of the tutors had done all or some of their teacher training in the former Catholic Colleges but few, if any, of the new teachers had done even some of their training in Catholic colleges or universities. They had trained in a great variety of educational institutions and some entirely within the school environment. This has practical implications for the induction for new teachers and also for the training of our Induction Tutors. We may regret these changes, we may constructively criticise many aspects of these recent developments, but we have to live with them unless we can change Government policy.

It is up to all of us to ensure that we uphold the distinctive features of what we believe to be sound education inspired and challenged by our faith in the unique dignity of every human being and in the achievement of their full potential. This may call for real and open dialogue with the Government, other educational establishments and also with the diversity we may find in the staff. We may well need to be critical of what we see as endangering this sound education based on Christian principles. We should support our Catholic and Christian universities by encouraging students who want to teach to attend them and be open to school based teacher training in good Catholic and other schools. However, we should see to it that all new members of staff have a sound grounding in what may be asked of them if they choose to be an active member of the educating community of a Catholic school. We should also encourage those teaching for some years to follow the various courses which the universities and some dioceses offer on leadership in Catholic schools. This is becoming essential for those who aspire to leadership in Catholic schools.

A crisis that is also potential and challenge

Recently I was discussing the issue of Catholic schooling with some colleagues, diocesan advisers, who said that they thought we were in danger of losing our schools. I assumed they were referring to the attacks by those outside the Church who argue that our schools are elitist, not serving true social cohesion, and an unnecessary burden on the tax payer. However, it was the opinion of these colleagues that we would lose our schools because the new generation of teachers had, on the whole, little knowledge of the faith and of the Catholic mission of our schools consequently they would lose their very reason for existing. While I could not entirely agree with the rather sweeping comment about the faith or commitment of the new generation of teachers, I could accept that we had to address what is clearly a major challenge of our post-modern culture which affects us all, especially the younger generation, and of the fact that our resources for preparing new teachers for Catholic schools are much reduced. The challenge is to assess what resources are available and develop them further. It is vitally important that we give our full attention and care to the recruitment and retention of teachers and the induction and training process which takes account of where they are in their own faith, professional life and career. We have a duty to support them and enable them actively to contribute to the educating community which is the hallmark of our schools. No general assumptions can be made about the ability or confidence of all teachers to engage students in their faith journey, in the religious and spiritual aspects of every subject of the curriculum and in what the school stands for. Nor can it be simply assumed that they are uninterested or unwilling to assist in this task; with support and advice, they can better understand what is expected of them in the educating community of the school. They often hold certain basic human values which are also central to our Christian beliefs. Often they are keen to play their part by making use of their talents and expertise in, for example, music, art, drama. As with the students and their families there is a huge spectrum of practice and commitment among teachers. This calls for the sensitive encouragement and support of chaplains, the head of RE, induction tutors and the leadership team, and especially the head.

We constantly speak of our schools as a 'faith community' but we have to be careful with the term 'faith community' since all are not of the same Catholic faith. There is diversity among students and staff. This can be enriching if all members of staff work together as a team, as an educating community. In our Catholic schools we have a double mandate: to educate in the faith, to educate inspired by faith.[86] There is the duty of articulating our Christian faith and of enabling students to come to a better understanding of that faith. However, as Pope Francis forcefully says, this must be done in a way that fully respects the conscience of all students and teachers. Pope John Paul II spoke of the proper balancing of this respect and duty.

> While Catholic establishments should respect freedom of conscience, that is to say avoid burdening consciences from without by exerting physical or moral pressure, especially in the case of the religious activity of adolescents, they still have the grave duty to offer religious training suited to the often widely varying religious situations of the pupils. [87]

We cannot expect all teachers to play an active part in educating in the faith to the same extent, but we can expect all to educate students inspired and challenged by the Christian faith vision. To achieve this we must give considerable time and energy to the important task of induction and training of all members of staff and also Governors to appreciate and uphold the Catholic ethos and mission of the school. Pope Francis stresses dialogue and the need to engage seriously in this 'qualified preparation' which is an on-going process of induction

---

[86] See Richard Shield's paper *Nurturing Spirituality and Vocation: A Catholic Approach to New Teacher Induction.* This is can be found on the website.

[87] John Paul II, Catechesis in Our Time, n. 69

and professional training and which cannot be satisfied with the initial induction of new teachers.

> The educator in Catholic schools must be, first and foremost, very competent, qualified and at the same time, rich in humanity, capable of being in the midst of young people with a pedagogical style, to promote their human and spiritual growth. Young people are in need of quality teaching, together with values not just enunciated but witnessed. [88]

The pope looks for teachers who are competent and qualified; he encourages us to continue to build on the qualifications they have in the teaching their subject areas and how they can actively contribute to the Christian ethos of the school. Much of that will be done by members of their own departments and by Induction Tutors. But all in the school are involved in helping them to become more competent in being with the young and promoting their human and spiritual growth by being themselves 'rich in humanity', showing their own human qualities and their liking and understanding of the young not just in words but by being 'witnesses'. That can be quite frightening to the young teacher but with support and good advice such qualities will soon blossom and make for the dedicated teacher. In his address to the Congregation for Catholic Education the pope stresses this ongoing training and qualification of teachers.

---

[88] Pope Francis, Address to the Congregation for Catholic Education, 2014 www.edinfo-centre.net

> We cannot improvise. We must engage seriously. In the meeting I had with General Superiors, I stressed that today education is addressed to a generation that changes; therefore, every educator – and the whole Church which is Mother Educator – is called to change, in the sense of being able to communicate with the young people she has before her...Because of this the educator is in need of permanent formation.

Easing, not adding to the burden of teachers.

There are a number of surveys and reports that speak of the burden of teaching which is expressed by all teachers, the recently qualified and those with many years in teaching including the good and outstanding ones. They frequently complain of being tired, over worked, they feel very pressurised not only by Government demands, but by the expectations of parents and the wider public. They feel that their task is not fully appreciated and there is little respect for the profession. The Croner Head Teacher's Special report makes for uncomfortable reading.

> There is little doubt that the teaching profession has become increasingly challenging with an accelerating pace for change, more individual responsibility and constant pressure for higher levels of performance. Teaching is now recognised as one of the most stressful professions. Many schools appear to create a 'pressure cooker' environment as they strive to raise academic

standards and meet increasingly demanding externally imposed targets. [89]

Pope Francis makes frequent mention of the amount of work expected of teachers as does the latest Vatican document.

> Teaching is not simply a job but a vocation that we must encourage. Nowadays teachers have to deal with an increasing number of tasks...Plus teachers are not valued by society as they used to be, and their job has become more cumbersome because of increasing administrative duties. [90]

Achieving academic standards is necessary and praiseworthy but it should not create in schools a 'pressure cooker' environment where constant pressure from above, from Head Teachers and Senior Management, driven by Government and inspection demands, is relentless and insensitive to the feelings and professionalism of teachers. Such an approach is hardly seeking to create that sense of community constantly stressed in all the Vatican documents and by Pope Francis as the hallmark of any Catholic school worthy of the name. As much time and effort should be spent on running a truly happy ship of educators who feel supported by all in the school, particularly by those in leadership roles as is spent on attaining achievement of academic standards and meeting Government targets. There will be times when greater efforts on raising standards by all are necessary, but not at the price of the

---

[89] Croner Head Teacher's Special report Issue no.58, 20 May, 20 May 2002

[90] *Educating Today and Tomorrow* p.13

loss of trust and friendship, of contentment in the job, which is part of the 'witness' the school gives to the younger generation. This can be a delicate balance.

> The complex network of interpersonal relations is the school's real strength, when it expresses love of truth, and teachers must be supported, so that they might provide the leaven and benevolent power to edify the community. In order for this to happen, particular attention must be devoted to the formation and selection of school heads. School heads must be leaders who make sure that education is a shared and living mission, who support and organise teachers, who promote mutual encouragement and assistance. [91]

Selection of Head Teachers and the Leadership Team

So it is that particular attention must be devoted to the training and selection of Head Teachers and Leadership Teams in our schools. This is an essential part of the ongoing process of induction into the understanding and fulfilling in practice the tradition of integral education within the Catholic ethos or environment. It is also an increasing problem in England and Wales as very often we have to advertise several times for Head Teachers and Deputies in primary and secondary schools and colleges. Many possible candidates hesitate to apply for various reasons to take on such a mission. Are we doing enough to prepare candidates for this remarkable vocation and

---

[91] op. cit.p.II

mission to society and the Church? The head teacher is not only in charge of the school from the point of view of the Government but he or she also represents the person of the bishop in matters ecclesial for the pastoral care of students and the overall mission of the school to families and the community. For many this can be a daunting task with pressure that they prefer to do without. They may not see their standing in the Church to be strictly suitable or 'orthodox'. Perhaps we should undertake a survey of those who hesitate or are unwilling to take on such a vocation so that we may have a clearer idea of their reasons for not applying for the post; a survey of those who do apply and succeed in gaining the post asking what they found attractive and difficult. These surveys might provide us with much needed data. Those in the Leadership Team need training and support to work as a team with shared but distinctive responsibilities and to be able to support and encourage the teachers and all the staff to play an active part on the educating community of the Catholic school.

A friendly relationship with families

The educating community includes families especially those in difficulties and in need of support. There should be a friendly alliance between teachers and parents. The document points out that 'an increasing number of children have been wounded during childhood. Poor school performance is rising and requires a preventive kind of education, as well as specific training for teachers' [92] All of this highlights how crucial training is

---

[92] op. cit. p. 19

for teachers, managers, governors and all staff who have educational responsibilities especially head teachers. Responsibility for adequate support and care should be provided at institutional level 'with competent leaders showing the way, rather than bureaucrats'. Also stressed, as I have already quoted, is the fact that 'teachers, parents and school heads – together with students – make up a broad educational community'[93] We must work together to make this a reality, not just a talking point. Support for all who take on responsibilities in our schools, among them governors, is an essential and challenging part of the Church's mission. It is the duty of those who have leadership roles in each diocese: bishop, finance committees, school directors and school advisers. Nationally they must be supported and encouraged by the Bishops' Conference and the Catholic Education Service. For the work each of these does to develop and defend our Catholic schools we should express deep gratitude and encouragement and ask that they, as Pope Francis says, appreciate that Catholic Education is 'one of the most important challenges of the Church, committed today to carrying out the New Evangelisation in an historical and cultural context in constant transformation'.

Head teachers and others can find inspiration in the words of Pope Francis to teachers in Argentina.

> To promote a wisdom that implies knowledge, evaluation, and practice is an ideal worthy to preside over any educational undertaking.

---

[93] op. cit. p. II

Whoever can contribute something in this way to his community will have contributed to the collective happiness in an incalculable degree. And we Christians possess in Jesus Christ a principle of the fullness of wisdom that we do not have the right to restrict within our confessional space. The evangelisation which our Lord urges refers to nothing else: to share a wisdom that from the beginning was destined for all men and women of all times. Let us renew audaciously the ardour of the announcement, of the offer we know envelops deep searches, silenced by so much confusion, let us do it daily and try to reach everyone [94]

---

[94] *Education for Choosing Life* p. 49

PAUSE FOR REFLECTION

Do you have any strong opinions for or against academies, free schools and Catholic schools with a large percentage of students of other Christian traditions or of other faiths? Can you give your reasons?

Do you know where the members of your staff have qualified?

Does the induction of new staff cover adequately the mission and ethos of the school as Catholic in way that respects all?

Do those who are of other Christian traditions, of other faiths or none feel part of the educating community? Is this the case on in-service days when the Catholic ethos and mission is being discussed?

Is there encouragement for longer serving teachers to further and develop their professional skills and be prepared for added responsibilities within a Catholic environment?

Chapter Six

POPE FRANCIS ON EDUCATING FOR CHOOSING LIFE

> *Do not be downhearted in the face of the difficulties that the educational challenge presents! Education is not a profession but an attitude, a way of being. In order to educate it is necessary to step out of ourselves and be among young people, to accompany them in the stages of their growth and to set ourselves beside them. Give them hope and optimism for their journey in the world.*[95]
>
> *If we look at Jesus, the incarnate Wisdom God, we will be able to realise that difficulties become challenges, challenges call forth hope and generate happiness in knowing yourselves to be architects of something new. All this surely impels us to continue giving the best of ourselves.* [96]

The following are a series of reflections of Pope Francis with my comments on their relevance to my own experiences with teachers and students. These reflections are for the most part taken from various addresses to students and educators and especially from his book Education for Choosing Life: Proposals for Difficult Times. In this book he shared thoughts with educators in Argentina and although they deal with particular social,

---
[95] Pope Francis, Address to students of Jesuit Schools in Italy and Albania 2014
[96] Education for Choosing Life p. 43

political and economic problems, they also have a universal appeal and speak to us in our situation today. They are hopeful and optimistic reflections spoken by a pope who was himself a teacher and who fully recognises the importance of the mission of our schools in today's Church and society. The opening quotation for this chapter is from his address to students and teachers in Jesuit schools in Italy and Albania. He speaks eloquently of the 'attitude' of teachers who should willingly step out of themselves to be with young people as teachers who are also friends and adult companions and mentors in the significant stages of the growth of the young into the people they can be. This is the wonderful task and mission of the teacher to 'set ourselves beside them; give them hope and optimism for their journey in the world'. This takes up the message of Vatican II: 'We can justly consider that the future lies in the hands of those who are strong enough to provide coming generations with reasons for living and hoping.'[97] That would seem to be his constant teaching and also the message of his book *Education for Choosing Life*.

Creative learning rather than simply managing learning

Pope Francis is very much aware of the difficulties of teaching today and encourages us not to be downhearted. He reminds us of the special and unique possibility and opportunity given to teachers to help open the minds and hearts of children and young people to

---

[97] The Church in the Modern World n. 31

goodness and to the service of others, to change things for the better, to build a different and better world for themselves and others: 'it is a service to persons, to little ones, to persons that place themselves in our hands so that we can help them to become what they can be'[98] To educate for Pope Francis is 'much more than offering knowledge: it will help our children and young people to evaluate and contemplate it, to make it flesh.'[99] He is very much for creativity in education and against the rigid approach which settles for management of what is to be learnt by simply preparing our students for their place in our consumerist society:

> There is nothing worse than a Christian education that is conceived in uniformity and calculation, in 'sausage making fashion'...Our objective is not only to form 'useful individuals for society', but to educate persons that can transform it! [100]

Frequently we hear teachers lamenting the over stress on certain areas of the curriculum to the detriment of equally important areas such as music, sport, art, drama; they complain of the rather narrow, limited teaching of certain subjects to meet the requirements of tests in primary schools and of examinations in secondary schools. Too often the focus is on knowledge, the content to be learnt, while neglecting the values and truths, wonder and awe, to be discovered in all areas of

---

[98] Education for Choosing Life p.27

[99] op. cit. p. 47.

[100] op. cit. p. 66

the curriculum – science, english, maths, history, geography, biology, religious education and so on.

The pope is quite adamant that we should not 'allow the individualistic and competitive mentality rooted in our urban culture to end by colonising our schools as well.'[101] The 'production of results', he says, belongs to the field of industry and relies on control: 'a society that tends to convert a person into a marionette of production and consumption always opts for results. It needs control.'[102] In his somewhat colourful imagery of 'sausage making fashion' and a 'marionette of production and consumption' he makes his views very clear that education involves much more than mere instruction. While such talk may seem to speak of some very lofty ideal which may come across as more 'airy fairy' than real, it is based on our Gospel-inspired vision of the person and the purpose of human life.

> Why does the Church, why do Christian communities invest time, assets and energy in a task that is not directly religious? Why do we have schools? Would it be to exercise an influence on society, an influence from which we subsequently hope for some benefit? The only reason we engage in the field of education is the hope of a new humanity, in another possible world. It is the hope which springs from Christian wisdom. [103]

---

[101] op. cit. p. 28

[102] op. cit. p. 64,65.

[103] op. cit. p. 60.

And this he declares 'is not mere poetry'. It is a vision we can easily lose sight of as we go about a normal busy day in school with all the pressures of meeting academic demands, of meeting the needs of each of the students – the gifted students and those with special needs, of attending to the pastoral care of each student and perhaps their families, of keeping a balanced discipline in our classrooms, of being responsible for extra curricula activities, keeping up with the paper work, and the list could go on. Pope Francis is very conscious of these 'excessive demands': 'I know that you are having to carry on your shoulders not only that for which you are prepared, but also a multitude of explicit or tacit demands that exhaust you'[104] In all this busyness we can forget the main reason why we are teachers, for our choosing to be educators of children and young people.

> Before the plans and the curricula, before defining the specific shape of codes and regulations, it is necessary to know what we want to generate. I also know that for this purpose the entire teaching community needs to involve itself, sharing forcefully in one self-same viewpoint becoming passionately committed to the project of Jesus and drawing everyone to the self-same side.

However this must be done in a pastoral tone and style and in language that is sensitive to the situation of all, committed Catholics and others. A number of years ago I facilitated an in-service days in a school on Catholic aspects of education. At the end of the day two teachers

---

[104] op. cit. p. 88

who were not Catholic thanked me for my reflections. They told me that they were very happy in the school and that they had important responsibilities but that on days when the Catholic aspect of the school was being discussed they felt somehow left out and not fully part of the team or educating community. On such occasions we must take care to appreciate the work of everyone and to make them feel that they are 'on the same side'. For that reason we should 'concentrate on the essentials, on what is most beautiful, most grand, most appealing and at the same time necessary' and enables every member of staff 'without exemption or exclusion' to feel that they have an active part in the mission of the school which becomes 'all the more forceful and convincing'.

The importance of creating a sense of community among staff and students

Facilitating such days of in-service or days of reflection will require of those who do the facilitating qualities that are respectful of and sensitive to all taking part in them. Thus giving a generous and appreciative recognition of the part everyone can and does play in creating and developing the educating community within the school [105] Each one of us adds to or detracts from this welcoming, supportive and collaborative ethos. In this matter we cannot be neutral. By our attitude – negative or positive - to students and members of staff, we enrich or impoverish the educating community. We cannot simply sit back and leave that to others while we do our obligatory teaching periods and enjoy our well-earned

---

[105] See my book *Serving the Young* pp. 41 -42 where I talk of 'An Educating Community'

breaks in the staff room. Pope Francis reminded the teachers of Jesuit schools in Italy and Albania: 'You are all educators there are no delegates in this field. Thus collaboration in a spirit of unity and community among the various educators is essential and must be fostered and encouraged'. This is aptly summed up in two of the Vatican documents.

> The school must be a community whose values are communicated through the inter-personal relationships of its members and through the individual and corporate adherence to the outlook on life that permeates the school. [106]

> It must never be forgotten that the school is always in the process of being created, due to the labour brought to fruition by all who have a role to play in it, and most especially by those who are teachers. [107]

Since Vatican II it is customary, as I have said, to speak of Catholic schools as 'communities' rather than 'institutes'. In the course of Section 48 Inspections I was always extremely pleased to hear students describe the atmosphere in their school as being 'like a family'. Students are very appreciative of the time and help they receive from staff and the good camaraderie among students. In the best schools when there is bullying they know the staff they can talk to and be confidant that action will be taken. Students know which members of

---

[106] The Catholic School n.32.

[107] Lay Catholics in School no. 78

staff they can go for a listening ear and help and support in times of difficulties or crisis.

Many years ago Bishop Konstant and I addressed a large group of teachers. The bishop spoke first and I followed him and was conscious that someone in the audience was clearly none too pleased with what he was hearing. As soon as we finished he quickly raised his hand and asked in a rather stern fashion 'I want to know what makes a Catholic school a Catholic school'. I was somewhat relieved when he wanted the bishop to answer. I am not sure that such was the answer he was expecting but I have never forgotten the bishop's reply: 'I suppose I would have to say some sense of belonging. If I do not feel happy being here much of what is done will simply go over my head, pass me by'. His words spoke volumes of the importance of creating the right welcoming, supportive and homely, friendly atmosphere that should be experienced in all our schools. Pope Francis makes the same point even more forcefully and gives reasons for our creating community in the school:

> Very rightly we put the accent on community life, on amplifying our capacity for welcoming and stability, in creating human ties and environments of happiness and love which permit our children and young people to grow and bear fruit. And we do well in doing so: so many times these basic contributions are denied them by a society which is even harder and success-driven, competitive, individualistic. [108]

---

[108] Education for Choosing Life, p. 47

School should be for all students a safe and caring place. It is vital that new members of staff, as well as our children and young people, experience this welcoming and supportive help from those who have been in the school for some time, especially from the Senior Leadership Team, from members of their departments and those involved in the induction process. We need the energy, keenness and ideas of new members of staff. They have much to offer. We should not be too judgemental or critical or over defensive of the status quo. We should discover and build on their talents and good qualities which they offer to the school. What Pope Francis says to teachers about their dealings with students can also be applied to the way we relate to other teachers, especially those new to the school.

> I invite you to find ways of generating enthusiasm in our young people for the enormous transformative potential that lies within their grasp, not so much through harangues and discourses but rather bringing them together to develop experiences and concrete situations that permit them to discover their own abilities. [109]

The pope sees this as important for all, students and teachers, especially those new to the school. He encourages us to find ways of generating enthusiasm not so much through 'harangues and discourses' but rather bringing them together and enabling them to develop experiences which permit them 'to discover their own abilities'. This is essential in educating the young in

---

[109] op. cit. p 113.

primary and secondary schools – to generate enthusiasm in them. It is equally important in our relationship with new members of staff. Newly qualified teachers are for the most part themselves young people who have chosen the vocation of teaching, who are keen and eager to learn and we should be prepared in whatever way we can to support them and walk with them on this gradual journey: 'bringing them together to develop experiences and concrete situations that permit them to discover their own abilities'. We should not expect the finished product or assume on their part complete understanding of how the ethos of the school is actually experienced in all that is done in the life of the school. If we wish a secure future for our schools then we must patiently journey with and be supportive of our younger and new colleagues.

The school serves the wider community

The pope reminds us that schools serve the neighbourhood and the families of our students, remember his challenging question: 'Do we believe in our pupils, in the families of our neighbourhood, in our people?'[110]

> We try to take the pulse of the times in which we live, and try to understand how we can recreate our spiritual experience in a way that responds to the questions, anxieties and hopes of our times. This effort is indispensable. [111]

---

[110] op. cit. p.35.

[111] op. cit. p. 83.

This statement is reminiscent of the opening paragraph of *The Church in the Modern World*:

> The joys and hopes, the grief and anguish of people of our time, especially of those who are poor or afflicted, are the joys and hopes, the grief and anguish of the followers of Christ as well. Nothing that is genuinely human fails to find an echo in their hearts'.

The school cannot exist in splendid isolation; we cannot simply take in children and young people and close the door on the world in which they live. Much as some of us might like to give our lessons in academically sealed classrooms; students bring with them their experiences, good and bad, of family life and the life of the locality in which they live. They bring with them anxieties, real fears and hopes. Pope Francis states very clearly 'I believe it is critical to try to approach the reality these children live in our society and ask ourselves what role we play in it.'[112] Educators need to be very much aware of this as they seek to deal with the pastoral care of students. A Vatican document reminds us strongly of this aspect of our mission:

> In spite of many obstacles, the Catholic school has continued to share responsibility for the social and cultural development of different communities and peoples to which it belongs, participating in their joys and hopes, their sufferings and difficulties, their efforts to achieve genuine human and communitarian progress. In this respect, mention

---
[112] op. cit. p. 85

> must be made of the invaluable services of the Catholic school to the spiritual and material development of people who are less fortunate.[113]

This applies to our so-called 'developed' world – our world – as it does to countries of the 'developing' world. Special mention is made in the same Vatican document of 'the unpretentious yet caring and sensitive help offered in those cases, more and more numerous above all in wealthy nations, of families which are fragile or have broken up'. At the end of the first chapter I quoted from the Vatican document *The Catholic School on the Threshold of the Third Millennium.* It speaks dramatically of young people to whom no values are proposed, who come from families which are broken and incapable of love, who live in situations of material and spiritual poverty, who face a future of unemployment and marginalisation. It ends with the great promise which is part of Pope Francis's dream 'to these new poor the Catholic school turns in a spirit of love'

Young people have a capacity to feel the suffering of others.

The pope acknowledges that

> Young people have an enormous capacity to feel the suffering of their neighbour and give themselves body and soul to action. This social

---

[113] The Catholic School on the Threshold of the Third Millennium n.5

sensibility, often merely emotional, should be educated towards a solidarity of depth.[114]

Students in our schools willingly and generously undertake a number of projects for the service of others: those suffering from cancer, those suffering from child abuse, the homeless and migrants, help for schools in poorer countries. The pope is insistent that it should not only be a matter of fund raising and feeling good about it. It must go deeper than that, they should be aware of the reasons why they do it; and in doing so they actively help those in greater need and play a part in making the world a better place. Addressing students on this issue he reflects on the two fundamental values: freedom and service:

> Freedom means being able to think about what we do, being able to assess what is good and what is bad, these are the types of conduct that lead to development; it means opting for the good. Let us be free to choose goodness. And in this do not be afraid to go against the tide, even if it is not easy. Always being free to choose goodness is demanding but it will make you people with backbone who can face life, people with courage and patience.
>
> In your schools you take part in various activities that accustom you to not retreating into yourselves but rather being open to others, especially the poorest and neediest. They accustom you to working hard to improve the

---

[114] Education for Choosing Life p.114

world in which we live. Be men and women with others and for others: true champions at the service of others. [115]

This should be an essential hallmark of our schools and a committed response to Pope Francis' appeal for 'a poor Church for the poor' – an appeal which speaks to all people who wish to improve the plight of men, women and children who lack the necessities of life, who are deprived of peace and justice and the acknowledgement of their basic human rights.

> To educate for solidarity supposes not only teaching to be good and generous, to take up collections, to participate in public good works, to support foundations and NGOs. It is precisely to create a new mentality that thinks in terms of community, of the priorities of the lives of all and each one above the appropriation of goods by a few. [116]

This education for fraternal solidarity is a constant theme of Pope Francis and should be an essential part of the education we seek to provide in our schools: 'this must be the distinctive seal of all and each of its dimensions and activities'.[117] In this we will find useful teaching resources in the publications of CAFOD adapted and suitable to all ages from children in primary school to older students in secondary school and sixth forms.

---

[115] Address to students of Jesuit schools in Italy and Albania.

[116] *Education for Choosing Life* p.70.

[117] op. cit. p. 27

The value of dialogue in our multi-cultural, multi-religious society

In his address to the Congregation for Catholic Education the pope puts great stress on respect and dialogue acknowledging that

> Catholic schools and universities are frequented by many non-Christian students and even non-believers. The Catholic educational institutions offer to all an educational proposal that looks to the integral development of the person and that responds to the right of all to accede to learning and knowledge. However, all equally are called to offer – with full respect for each one's liberty and of the methods proper to the school environment – the Christian proposal, namely Jesus Christ as the meaning of life, the cosmos and of history.

He encourages 'encounter and dialogue with courageous and innovative fidelity which will make the Catholic identity meet with the different spirits of the multi-cultural society'. When speaking to the students of Jesuit schools in Albania he was full of praise for their openness 'after long years of repression of religious institutes to accepting and educating Catholics, Orthodox and Muslim children as well as several pupils born into agnostic culture. The school is becoming a place for dialogue and serene exchanges to encourage attitudes of respect, listening, friendship and a spirit of collaboration'.

While this may seem more appropriate to schools in certain countries, in India, Pakistan, Albania and elsewhere, it is increasingly an issue for schools in Britain and one that we can no longer ignore.[118] We can and must learn from the experiences of Catholic educators in these countries. Our Catholic schools are a precious means of contributing to the progress of the Church and society in today's multi-cultural and multi-faith and secular society.

These are some of the key issues which Pope Francis highlights in his various talks and writings and some of the qualities he sees as being essential in teachers and educators within our schools. There are no doubt others which the reader may wish to stress in reading Pope Francis's thoughts and reflections which are quite radical. I have offered these in the hope that they may inspire and challenge us as we seek to educate coming generations 'for choosing life'. I conclude with his reflection made in his address to the Congregation for Catholic Education in February 2014 some of which I have already quoted.

> To educate is an act of love. It is to give life. And love is demanding, it calls for using the best resources, for awaking passion and to begin with patience together with young people. The educator in Catholic schools must be, first of all, very competent, qualified and, at the same time, rich in humanity, capable of being in the midst of young people with a pedagogical style, to promote their

---

[118] See *Meeting God in Friend & Stranger*, Catholic Bishops' Conference of England & Wales, 2010.

human and spiritual growth. Young people are in need of quality teaching, together with values not just enunciated but witnessed. Coherence! We cannot make them grow; we cannot educate them without coherence: coherence, witness.

PAUSE FOR REFLECTION

What do you find most impressive, most challenging in Pope Francis' teaching on Catholic education?

How much of teachers' time is be taken up with managing learning rather than on creative learning? What is the value of creative learning? How is this achieved in your school?

The Pope places great stress in creating a sense of community among staff and students, what importance does the school put on this and in what ways and why?

In what ways do the students serve the needs of the wider community? How does the school encourage students to be 'true champions at the service of others'?

Do you see the need and the value of dialogue which encourages attitudes of respect, listening, friendship and a spirit of collaboration? How is this encouraged in your school?

Chapter Seven

BENEDICT XVI's VISIT TO BRITAIN - REFLECTIONS ON CATHOLIC EDUCATION

One of the great challenges facing us today is how to speak convincingly of the wisdom and liberating power of God's word to a world which all too often sees the Gospel as a constriction of human freedom, instead of the truth which liberates our minds and enlightens our efforts to live wisely and well, both as individuals and as members of society [119].

We live in a celebrity culture, and young people are often encouraged to model themselves on figures from the world of sport or entertainment. My question for you is this: what are the qualities you see in others that you would most like to have yourselves? What kind of person would you really like to be? [120]

We no doubt remember the remarkably successful visit of the previous pope, Pope Benedict XVI, and of his reflections on Catholic education. At that time I talked about them in various inset days in dioceses and schools. It seems only fitting that I should include them in this text. Catholic education is a wide concept and should not be identified simply with Catholic schooling. It is a task in which we are all involved in home, parish and school,

---

[119] Homily in Westminster Cathedral

[120] Address to pupils at Mary's, Strawberry Hill

as parents, priests and teachers. However, Pope Benedict during his visit praised and valued the work that is being done in Catholic education in our schools for the young here in Britain. We were encouraged by Pope Benedict during his visit to celebrate nationally all that has been and is being achieved in Catholic education, particularly by dioceses, religious men and women, and by lay people, rich and poor, over many years before and after the restoration of the hierarchy in 1850.

Can and should we celebrate Catholic education in Britain Today?

Two years after the restoration of the hierarchy in 1852 the bishops of England and Wales boldly stated 'the first necessity is a sufficient provision of education adequate for the wants of the poor...prefer the establishment of a good school to every other work'. In the context of the times and especially of the large numbers of Irish immigrants in the aftermath of the great famine the stress was on meeting the needs of the poor and of offering them the opportunity to preserve the faith in an often hostile and very secular society. There are a number of Catholics who may wonder if we are still true to that mission and whether our present day endeavours are worthy of celebration. There are Catholics who believe that our schools are falling short at least in the vital mission of passing on the faith to the younger generation. The youthful presence or lack of it at Sunday Mass clearly makes many raise this question. Many others believe that we do carry on that same mission but in a world that is very different and in a Church 'which is indeed the same Church as before, but it is required and called to be the same Church as before very differently'.[121] In his homily in Westminster cathedral the Pope Benedict referred to the difficulty of speaking of the liberating Word of God in a culture which is indifferent and sees the truths of the Gospel as restricting human freedom.

The world of today's young is very different to the world we grew up in.

I often recall the story of the student who went for advice to Michael Paul Gallagher, a Jesuit, lecturing at the time in English and American literature in University College Dublin. The priest listened to what the student had to say and he began his response with the words 'When I was your age' when the student stopped him and said 'Father, you were never my age!' Michael Paul was taken aback then realised that the student was saying 'you were never nineteen in 2010'. It is important for us to stop and reflect on the world and Church we lived in when we were nineteen and critically and sympathetically compere it to the more complex culture of today's world. This has clear implications for schools as is clearly stated in a Vatican document already quoted.

> One must recognise that more than ever before the job of the Catholic school is infinitely more difficult, more complex, since this is a time when Christianity demands to be clothed in new

---

[121] N. Lash, Theology for Pilgrims, DLT, 2008, p.224

garments, when all manner of changes have been introduced in the Church and in secular life. And particularly, when a pluralist mentality can dominate and the Christian Gospel is increasingly pushed to the side-lines. [122]

It is when we reflect prayerfully on the complexities and difficulties which arise from this cultural background that we can appreciate the good done in our schools and also acknowledge the flaws and shortcomings. Benedict XVI in his talks in different parts of the country gave us some very sound advice on this point when reflecting on the education provided in our Catholic schools.

Looking at the Bigger Picture

Talking to the children and young people gathered in St. Mary's Strawberry Hill, Pope Benedict reminded them of what he called:

> The bigger picture over and above the subjects you study, the different skills you learn…Always remember that every subject you study is part of a bigger picture. The world needs good scientists, but a scientific outlook becomes dangerously narrow if it ignores the religious and ethical dimension of life, just as religion becomes narrow if it rejects the legitimate contribution of science to our understanding of the world.

---

[122] The Catholic School n. 66 -67.

He went on to say that we needed good historians, philosopher and economists and warned that they too should not be too narrow in their view of life. Benedict also acknowledged that not everyone in the school is of the Catholic tradition and said:

> I wish to include all of you in my words today. I pray that you too will feel encouraged to practise virtue and grow in knowledge and friendship with God alongside your Catholic classmates. You are a reminder to them of the bigger picture that exists outside the school, and indeed, it is only right that respect and friendship for members of other religious traditions should be among the virtues learned in a Catholic school.

Sense of Community and friendly relationships

One of the experiences that young people who attended the various events with Pope Benedict spoke most enthusiastically about was being together with so many other young people and people of all ages. The community dimension of school is much appreciated by students. They speak highly of their companionship with other students and of the helpful and friendly relationships with many teachers. When talking to students in the course of inspections they frequently highlight this aspect – 'It is like a family' is a frequent remark. In his address to the young people in Strawberry Hill the Pope Benedict said

Indeed, the life of faith can only be effectively nurtured when the prevailing atmosphere is one of respectful and affectionate trust. I pray that this will continue to be as a hallmark of schools in this country.

I believe it is a hallmark of most of our schools and one we should not overlook. A Vatican document declares that the community dimension 'is one of the most enriching developments for the contemporary school'[123] In our schools students are also given the opportunity to take on all sorts of responsibilities in the school: as members of the School Council, as prefects and mentors to younger students, as members of the anti-bullying campaign and in many other activities which serve the needs of fellow students and others beyond the school.

We are made to receive love; we are made to give love

Outside Westminster cathedral he eloquently reminded the young people that

> We are made for love...we were made to receive love and we have from all those people in our lives who have helped us to realise how precious we are in their eyes and in the eyes of God.

Benedict enumerated a number of such people including friends, parents, teachers and others. That is an important part of the vocation of the educator: to help all young people see 'how precious they are' in their

---
[123] The Catholic School on the Threshold of the Third Millennium n.18

teachers' eyes and the eyes of God. He then went on to say that 'we are made to give love. Every day we have to choose love and this requires help'. Such help is given by many teachers who enable students to fulfil their unique potential and to find their true place in life, to fulfil that 'definite service' or 'mission' that God has in mind for each one. This refers to the understanding of our unique vocation and of our God given mission in the world expressed by Cardinal John Henry Newman whom he beatified during his visit. At Strawberry Hill Benedict posed this question 'what sort of person would you really like to be?' He urged young people to respond to God's love 'by reflecting something of his infinite goodness'. He spelt out some ways that they could do this:

- Avoiding destructive and dangerous tendencies that cause suffering and damage.
- Feeling compassion for people in difficulties, being ready to help.
- Coming to the aid of the poor and hungry.

As I have noted elsewhere, one of the most impressive aspects of Catholic schools today is the great amount of fund-raising for various charitable causes both locally and globally. The students not only give a good deal but are very aware of why they do so. While they thus try to enrich the life of others, they enrich their own. This is an important dimension of our Christian faith which the young in our schools are very much engaged.

Time for silence and reflection

Pope Benedict reminded the young people that this 'requires moments of silence...because it is in silence that we find God and in silence we discover ourselves'. The young find silence difficult. They are constantly bombarded by noise, loud music; they are forever on their phones and all the other technical machines they carry around. Silence is in short supply! Yet in my experience the good Catholic school addresses this call of Pope Benedict. There are well prepared and creative acts of collective worship with power point and music which allow for prayer and silence as they reflect on issues that are topical and speak to the young. However, teachers can tend to talk too much and over use the power point; they should allow for some silent reflection on the students' part so that they can take the message to heart and see implications for their lives. Most schools now have a chapel or quiet room and chaplains often introduce them to various forms of meditation and prayer. The liturgical year is marked by special services. In form time each day there is the opportunity for a brief reflective prayer and silence this helps settle students down as they pray for loved ones, those in need, or reflect on topics of relevance to them and. This is, of course, something which Heads, chaplains and advisers need to oversee and ensure that it takes place.

Help for Families

Pope Benedict did not really mention this feature of school life during his visit. However, he did stress the need to support families in many of his other talks. He certainly stressed it forcefully to the Salesians gathered in Rome for our 26th General Chapter. I quote this passage in full since it reminds us that we cannot separate our mission to young people from or support and care for their families.

> In the education of youth it is extremely important that the family play an active role. Families frequently have difficulty in facing the challenges of education; they are often unable to make their contribution or are absent. The special tenderness of Don Bosco's charism must be expressed in equal commitment to the involvement and formation of families. Your youth ministry, therefore, must be decisively open to family ministry. Caring for families does not mean taking people away from work with young people; on the contrary, it means making it more permanent and effective. I thus encourage you to deepen the forms of this commitment on which you have set out; this will prove advantageous to the education and evangelisation of the young' [124]

The document The Catholic School on the Threshold of the Third Millennium also praises schools 'for the unpretentious yet caring and sensitive help offered in those cases, more and more numerous above all in wealthy nations, of families which are fragile or have broken up'. Our schools have close links with families, are aware of problems and seek to offer sensitive care. We need only ask Head Teachers and pastoral care staff.

---

[124] Acts of the 26th Salesian General Chapter p.125

The Pope's tone and language

Throughout the visit Pope Benedict addressed his advice and challenges to the young and their educators by way of invitation, not in a judgemental or overly negative tone. He addressed their aspirations and ideals. Young people turned out in their thousands, many schools sending a large delegation of students to the various events. They were deeply impressed, thoroughly enjoyed the experience and were deeply moved. We can, however, be fairly sure that not all of them attend Mass every Sunday. However, he made them think seriously about what they are doing with their lives and challenged them to live the Gospel and to think seriously about following Christ and being of service to those in need. Our Catholic schools in addressing the many needs of the young in the context of today's secular culture and indifference to religion seek to do the same. The former Bishop of Shrewsbury Brian Noble spoke of the need of 'keeping alive the rumour of God' in our Catholic schools. In many ways that is what we strive to do and we should not be too negative or judgemental of what we see as their success or failure. The staff and students could do with our praise and encouragement.

PAUSE FOR REFLECTION

Did any groups from your school have the opportunity to meet Pope Benedict during his visit? How did students react to the visit?

Is there time for reflective, prayerful silence in the school day?

Does the act of worship include participation of students and does it encourage reflection and prayer?

Is there a chapel or quiet room in the school; how are staff and students encouraged to make good use of it?

How can the school work more closely with families and parishes?

Chapter Eight

POPE FRANCIS AND DON BOSCO'S SYSTEM OF EDUCATION

May Don Bosco's experience and his 'preventive system' sustain you always in your commitment to live with the young people. May your presence in their midst be distinguished by that tenderness that Don Bosco called affection, experiencing also new languages, knowing well that the language of the heart is the fundamental one to get close to them and to become their friends. [125]

The world will always welcome us as long as all our concern is for the under-developed people, for poor children, for those members of society most in danger. This is our real wealth which no one will envy and no one will take from us. [126]

Pope Francis is a Jesuit but he has connections with other religious congregations. Among these are the Salesians of Don Bosco. His grandparents Giovanni and Rosa together with his father Mario Jose emigrated from Piedmont, northern Italy, which was also the birthplace

---

[125] Pope Francis address to the members of the Salesian 27th General Chapter 2013.

[126] From The Spiritual Testament of St. John Bosco, Salesian Constitutions p. 269

of Don Bosco. He attended the San Juan Bosco primary school run by the Salesian sisters. In the sixth grade he was a student in a Salesian college for some time. The San Lorenzo football club of which he is a great fan was founded by a Salesian priest, Fr. Lorenzo Massa, in order to provide for the lads of the area some useful activity and to keep them safe and out of trouble. In his teenage years he had a Salesian spiritual director, Fr. Enrique Pozzoli, who also baptised him. He thought of becoming a Salesian at one time. He was even accused of 'Salesianising' the Jesuit province by some of his fellow Jesuits because of his close association with the Salesians before entering the Jesuits. Over the years as a Jesuit and later as Archbishop he would meet many Salesians who are numerous in Argentina and Latin America. As Pope he addressed the members of the Salesian 27th General Chapter and showed that he had knowledge and appreciation of the system of education inspired by Don Bosco and he encouraged and challenged the whole Salesian family to continue and develop it to meet the many needs of young people today.

The inspiration: the dream at the age of nine

The inspiration for his work can be found in a dream which the young John Bosco had at the age of nine. This dream remained in his memory and only gradually did he come to understand its full message and its real significance for his life's work with and for young people. In his dream John was playing with his friends in the local village. A quarrel started among the lads. He rushed in to try to stop it with his fists flying. Suddenly a man of dignified appearance was present and rebuked him: 'No not like that; rather you will calm them and win them over with kindness and gentleness'. Later in the dream a lady appeared took him by the hand and then said: 'this is the field of your labour. Make yourself humble, determined and strong. You must do for my sons what you now see happen to these animals'. There were a large number of fierce animals; then they disappeared and he saw gentle lambs, all frisking about. He began to cry and asked the lady to speak clearly since he did not know what all this meant. She then placed her hand on his head and said: 'In good time you will understand everything'.

Don Bosco began his work In Turin. Between 1814 and 1848 the population of the city doubled mainly due to the influx of many young people who flocked to the city in search of work. This inevitably led to overcrowding, homelessness, poverty, hunger, rowdiness and criminal activity. Don Bosco as a young priest was very sensitive to the needs of these young people who he met on the streets and in his visits to prisons. He began to gather young lads on a Sunday for catechism class and then for fun and games. Eventually after many hardships and trials he founded the Oratory or Youth Centre at Valdocco which gradually became a hostel, a trade school, a secondary school, a place where the youngster could meet and recreate. Very quickly he gathered a group of helpers and was joined by some priests, many men and women, good lay folk, eager to help the young people. In the 1850s he ensured the continuation of his work by founding the Salesian Society. His first Salesians were mainly from his more mature students. In a remarkably short time the work spread in Europe, in Argentina and throughout Latin America and elsewhere. He was no theoretician or author of a complete educational treatise. He was a man of great common sense who was moved by concern for the young and inspired to meet their needs in a way that they would respond to. Today the Salesian Family consisting of Salesians priests, brothers and sisters, lay men and women, volunteers of various ages, work in schools and colleges, youth centres, centres for street kids, for those on the margins of society, and those in great need all over the world. However, the educational approach is always the same, the preventive system inspired by Don Bosco.

The Preventive System

The Pope in his address to the General Chapter speaks of the 'preventive system' of Don Bosco which is the heart of all his educational endeavours. Don Bosco wrote in the regulations for the Salesians that there are two distinct systems of education: 'the preventive and the repressive'. According to the repressive system 'the words and looks of the superior must always be severe and even threatening, and he must avoid all familiarity with his dependents'. He sees the preventive system to be 'quite different from this and I might say even opposed to it':

It consists in making the laws and regulations of an institute known, and then watching carefully so that the pupils may at all times be under the vigilant eye of the Rector or assistants, who like loving fathers can converse with them, take the lead in every moment and in a kindly way give advice and correction.

At the heart of all this is, as the Pope says, being present in their midst, assistance, accompaniment, standing with them, walking with them with real affection. In the mind of Don Bosco the word preventive is far richer than preventative. It means the ability to be a step ahead of the young people, reading their needs before they become aware of them, and being there to give them the encouragement to succeed.[127]

It means that we are not simply seen as teachers in the classroom but can mix with them in the corridors, in the playground, during the dinner hour, in extra curriculum activities and other times. The aim is not simply to prevent trouble or supervise them but to know them better and as adult friends to be ready with advice and encouragement when necessary. With regard to rewards or punishment Don Bosco used to say 'praise for work well done and blame for carelessness are already a reward or punishment'. Don Bosco maintained that except in very rare cases, punishment should 'never be given publicly but always in the absence of companions; and the greatest prudence and patience should be used

[127] D. O' Malley, Ordinary Ways, Don Bosco Publications

to bring the pupil to see his or her fault, with the aid of reason and religion'. He advised that we should not punish when angry but take time to cool down before speaking to the one who offended and caused such anger. He was utterly against all forms of corporal punishment.

Three pillars: reason, religion and loving kindness

The preventive system he frequently declared 'is based entirely on reason, religion, and above all kindness'; these were words constantly on his lips. Taken together in a balanced way they are the very basis of his whole educational system, his preventive system. Teachers should always be **reasonable** with students and explain 'the reasons for their direction or guidance. They should attempt to show that it is for the student's own good, to make them a better person, a richer, more mature and likeable human being. There were to be no harsh rules or sanctions; these more often than not turn the students against their educators and left them with unhappy, angry memories. The motivation is found in **religion** and is based on the words of St. Paul: 'Love is patient and kind...Love bears all things ...hopes all things, endures all things.' In his Oratory or Youth Centre students were encouraged to take the opportunity to celebrate the sacraments and to take part in the main feasts of the liturgical year but always in a joyful, festive spirit that spoke to the young. Don Bosco actually said 'hence only a Christian can apply the preventive system'. Yet in many Salesian schools and other schools inspired by his educational approach, many of the educators and students are of other faiths such as Hindu, Sikh and Muslim. Together with Salesians and Christian lay people they can see the appeal of Don Bosco's system and what Pope Francis calls 'the essential, what is more beautiful, most grand' in education. In many Salesian schools and other works many of the students and those in care are not Christian but are from other faiths and none. This wider view of religion has something to offer to them all.

The heart of all this is above all **kindness**, a deep respect for each young person, a familiarity with all that appeals to them, having their interests and needs very much at heart, being always welcoming and friendly, willing to listen and being happy in their company, showing trust in them. The Pope speaks highly of the Salesian presence among the young which is 'distinguished by that tenderness that Don Bosco called affection knowing well that the language of the heart is the fundamental one to get close to them and become their friends'. The Salesians respond in Don Bosco's preventive system to the Pope's exhortation to teachers in Buenos Aires already quoted.

> I invite you to find ways of generating enthusiasm in our young people for the enormous transformative potential that lies in their grasp, not so much through harangues and discourses but rather bringing them together to develop experiences and concrete situations that permit them to discover their own abilities.[128]

---

[128] *Education for Life* p. 113

Four overlapping elements: home, school, parish and playground

In our Salesian constitutions we read that Don Bosco lived a pastoral experience in his first Oratory or Youth Centre which serves as a model for all Salesian activities: 'The oratory was for the youngsters a home that welcomed, a parish that evangelised, a school that prepared them for life, and a playground where friends could meet and enjoy themselves. [129] These four elements of home, parish, school and playground can be seen as the fourfold approach of any Salesian work, a school, a youth centre or a home for street kids.

It should be a **home**, a place where all are welcomed, feel happy there and have a real sense of belonging, of being part of a community, a family, where all have responsibilities and can play an active part; a place where they are trusted and respected, accepted as they are broken or whole, and not turned away when they make a mistake. The creation of a truly family spirit was the foundation of his approach to education. It is a **parish** where God can be worshipped in joyful, youthful services; where there is time for reflection on values and beliefs, for considering what is important in life and of being of service to others, especially those most in need, helping them to be good Christians, mature good living people. It is also a **school** which helps prepare the youngsters for life and its duties: family and civic duties and responsibilities and giving them the necessary

---

[129] Salesian Constitutions n.40

academic and technical resources to enable them to be 'honest citizens and earn their bread'. And it should be a **playground** where with friends and companions they can have fun, be joyful; providing a setting where the young people can be themselves, where relationships are formed between young people themselves and young people and their educators.

Don Bosco stressed that his students should keep a healthy balance between these four elements. If a student seemed to spend too much time in chapel and was not mixing enough with the others in the playground, Don Bosco would remind him that he should get together with the others and make friends, enjoy themselves and have some fun. Play he saw as essential to their full development. Equally he would encourage others who were for ever in the playground not to forget the chapel or their time for study best suited to their needs, academic work or learning a suitable trade. His oratory or youth centre was a place of joy, friendliness, and happiness, in a stimulating atmosphere which looked to the balanced, holistic education of all his young people.

His patron St. Francis of Sales

The name Salesian is taken from St. Francis of Sales, Don Bosco's patron, known for his gentle approach in his pastoral work which Don Bosco found relevant to his work for the young.

> He admired his joyful, optimistic spirituality and because of the gentleness of his approach, he chose him as patron of the Congregation. He wished his followers to be filled with the spirit of

> Francis of Sales- a kindness that was all embracing, a gentleness that was strong, a love that was humble and a faith that was steadfast. For Francis there was no religious elite; holiness was possible for everybody. Francis used a simple metaphor to sum up his work when he said: You catch more flies with a spoonful of honey than a barrel full of vinegar. In other words: love is stronger than violence or force of any kind.[130]

Don Bosco applied this to his pastoral work with the young: reason, religion and loving kindness. He held the ideal of holiness, as understood by Francis of Sales, as being possible for his boys; he inspired and encouraged many of them to try to achieve it while still at school doing the ordinary things of each day well, nothing exceptional like harsh penances and fasting. Chief among these school boys who lived a saintly, holy life was the fifteen year old St. Dominic Savio.

In our Salesian constitutions we read that

> Inspired by the optimistic humanism of St. Francis of Sales, the Salesian believes in people's natural and supernatural resources without losing sight of their weakness.
>
> He is able to make his own what is good in the world and does not bewail his own times; he accepts all that is good, especially if it appeals to the young.[131]

---
[130] J. Horan, Led by a Dream; The Salesian Story, p. 5

[131] Salesian Constitutions n.17

Educators should be optimistic and not 'bewail' or be over negative or condemnatory of the times;they should seek to accept what is good in the culture which appeals to the young, remembering and taking to heart the student's reply to Michael Paul Gallagher 'You were never my age!'

The bicentenary of his birth

There is a good deal more that should be said to do justice to Don Bosco as educator and of his outstanding life and pastoral work. This can be found in other texts and no doubt much more will be written as we celebrate the bicentenary of his birth in August 2015. What has been said here will suffice for the purpose of this text which is mainly concerned with celebrating the fiftieth anniversary of the Vatican II Declaration on Christian Education and addressed to those with responsibilities for our Catholic schools. We Salesians will celebrate the anniversary by courageously facing the challenges set for us by Pope Francis at our last chapter. The Pope encouraged the Salesian Family to be faithful to Don Bosco's work for poor and abandoned youth. To the members of the chapter he very forcefully said:

> We think of the vast reality of unemployment, with so many negative consequences. We think of dependencies, which unfortunately are multiple, which deprive from common roots of a lack of true love. To go against the marginalisation of young people requires courage, maturity and much prayer.

He then urged that 'the best must be sent to this work! The best!' So we Salesians will strive to respond to that call of the Pope and the theme of the chapter 'Witnesses of Evangelical Radicalism'. We will also strive to develop the mission in our schools again in response to Pope Francis in his address to the recent General Chapter.

> The evangelisation of young people is the mission that the Holy Spirit has entrusted to you in the Church. It is closely connected with their education: the journey of faith and the Gospel also enriches human maturation. Young people must be prepared to work in society according to the spirit of the Gospel, as agents of justice and peace, and to live as protagonists of the Church. Therefore, you avail yourselves of the necessary further pedagogical and cultural reflections and updating to respond to the present educational emergency'.

All of us who are involved as educators or administrators in our schools can apply this message of Pope Francis to our own lives and work.

PAUSE FOR REFLECTION

What do find most attractive in Don Bosco's system of education?

What do you think might be most difficult to put into practice for teachers? Why?

Would you say that your school was more 'preventive' than 'repressive' in its ethos and discipline?

How do the features of reason, religion and loving kindness feature in your school?

What do you understand by the blending of the elements of home, school, church and playground? How do they play a part in the education provided in your school?

Chapter Nine

SOME CONCLUSIONS AND QUALITY MARKS

Pope Francis reminds us that 'Catholic education is one of the most important challenges for the Church, committed today to carrying out the New Evangelisation in an historical and cultural context in constant transformation'. The quotations and reflections in this text provide truly inspirational and challenging insights to the essence and heart Catholic Education and New Evangelisation. I only hope that these quotations and my reflections on these insights and have helped convey something of the challenges and the radical recommendations outlined in the documents and in thoughts of Pope Francis and others. From time to time there may have been some repetitions of themes expressed with a slightly different nuance; this only shows how much these significant people and documents stress the importance of that particular feature of Catholic education.

By way of conclusion in the light of these insights I enumerate a number of the main 'quality marks' which have been highlighted in the documents and the thoughts of Pope Francis, of Pope Benedict and of Don Bosco. They speak of some of the distinctive features of the Catholic education which we should seek to ensure are not only talked about but actually lived in our schools and which should be the key features of the vocation and mission of all those who take up the wonderful challenge and grave responsibility of furthering and developing our Catholic schools.

Quality Marks inspired by the Church Documents

We should seek 'to express the living presence of the Gospel in the field of education, of science and of culture'.

The God given dignity of every human person is at the centre of all we do in Catholic education.

We seek to provide an education which is integral and holistic which seeks to enable each person to achieve his or her full potential.

We set great importance on creating a community, a sense of belonging and friendship among staff and students founded on the Gospel message of freedom and love.

The whole professional staff is called to present faith as 'an attractive option with a humble, supportive attitude'. The distinction between 'knowing and believing must always be respected'.

We recognise the importance of raising academic standards while acknowledging and respecting the professionalism and good will of most of the staff and striving to create a happy, contented educating community.

Staff should be respectful and supportive of the Head Teacher and those in leadership roles. They in turn must make sure that education is 'a shared and living mission' and 'promote mutual encouragement and assistance'.

We should ensure that we provide for the initial and permanent formation of all staff and Governors in promoting the Catholic ethos of the school in a way that is respectful and sensitive to all.

We should undertake respectful dialogue with others in our pluralist society; finding a language which appeals; not closing ourselves off in our Catholic world.

We should provide good pastoral care meeting the needs of individual students and families.

We take to heart the challenging question of Pope Francis 'Do we believe in our pupils, in the families of our neighbourhood, in our people?'

We strive to face the challenges of providing religious formation in our pluralist society in the spirit of St. Paul in Athens with respect and openness to dialogue.

We encourage students to undertake service of others in the school and in the wider community encouraging them to be 'true champions at the service of others'. Our objective is not only to form 'useful individuals for society but to educate persons that can transform it'.

We encourage and allow time for silence and reflection 'because it is in silence we find God and we discover ourselves'.

The care we provide for families does not detract us from working with the young 'it makes it more permanent and effective'.

We undertake a constant re-evaluation of what we do in our schools taking the recommendations and the guidelines outlined in the Vatican documents seriously.

Chapter Ten
WHY DOES THE CATHOLIC CHURCH HAVE SCHOOLS?

FINAL WORDS FROM POPE FRANCIS

'As Christians we are committed to the educational task, we have an important responsibility, and at the same time, an opportunity to make our contribution. For this reason, it is necessary to succeed in the objectives which are to be prioritised, based on a wisdom matured in experience of meeting with the Lord. For this purpose, it would not be superfluous to ask ourselves the fundamental question: for what purpose do we educate? Why does the Church, why do Christian communities, invest time, assets, and energy in a task that is not directly religious? Why do we have schools, and not hair salons, veterinary clinics, or tourist agencies? There will be those who think so, but the reality of many of our schools puts the lie to this affirmation. Would it be to exercise an influence in society from which we subsequently hope for some benefit?

It is possible that some schools offer this product to their clients: contacts, environment and excellence. But neither is this the reason for which the ethical and evangelical imperative pushes us to offer this service. The only reason we engage ourselves in the field of education is the hope for a new mankind, in another possible world.

It is the hope which springs from Christian wisdom, which in the Resurrected One reveals to us the divine stature to which we are called'[132].

'Despite the tide of secularism which has swept our societies, the Church is considered a credible institution by public opinion and, trusted for her solidarity and concern for those in greatest need...And how much good has been done by our schools and universities around the world! This is a good thing'[133].

Celebration and Challenge!

---

[132] Education for Choosing Life p.60

[133] Evangelii Gaudium n. 65

Appendix

DOCUMENTS OF THE CONGREGATION FOR CATHOLIC EDUCATION

The Catholic School 1977

Lay Catholics in School: Witnesses to Faith 1982

Educational Guidance on Human Love: Outlines for Sex Education 1983

The Religious Dimension of Education in a Catholic School 1988

The Catholic School on the Threshold of the Third Millennium 1997

Consecrated Persons and their Mission in Schools: Reflections and Guidelines 2002

Educating Together in Catholic Schools: A Shared Mission between Consecrated Persons and the Lay Faithful 2007

Educating to Intercultural Dialogue in Catholic Schools: Living in Harmony for a Civilisation of Love 2013

Educating Today and Tomorrow: A Renewing Passion 2014

PUBLICATIONS OF POPE FRANCIS

Evangelii Gaudium: Apostolic Exhortation on the Proclamation of the Gospel in Today's World, CTS, 2013

Educating for Choosing Life: Proposals for Difficult Times, Ignatius Press, San Francisco, 2014

PUBLICATIONS OF THE BISHOPS' CONFERENCE

Statement on Religious Education in Catholic Schools, 2000

Meeting God in Friend and Stranger: Fostering and Mutual Understanding between Religions, CTS, 2010

Religious Education Curriculum Directory 2012

PUBLICATIONS OF THE CATHOLIC EDUCATION SERVICE

Signposts and Homecomings, Report to Bishops' Conference, St Paul, 1981

Catholic Schools, Children of Other Faiths and Social Cohesion: Cherishing Education for Human Growth, Catholic Education Services 2008.

Catholic Education in England and Wales, Catholic Education Service, 2014

RELEVANT BOOKS AND RESOURCES

Ainsworth W. Don Bosco, The Man, The Priest, The Times. Don Bosco Publications

Gallagher J, Soil for the Seed: historical, pastoral and theological reflections on educating to and in faith, McCrimmons, Great Wakering, 2001.

Gallagher J, Serving the Young: Catholic Schools Today, Don Bosco Publications

Gallagher J, 'Are Our Schools Irreplaceable?', Pastoral Review Jan/Feb 2010

Gallagher J. 'Catholic Schools in England and Wales: New Challenges' in International Handbook of Catholic Education, G.R. Grace, J O'Keefe SJ (Eds.), Springer, Netherlands 2007, Part One p. 249-269.

Gallagher M. P. Clashing Symbols: An Introduction to Faith & Culture, DLT, 1997

Grace G. Catholic Schools: Mission, Market and Morality, Routledge Falmer, 2002

O'Malley W. What Happened at Vatican II, Harvard University Press, 2008

O'Malley D. Ordinary Ways, Don Bosco Publications.

O'Malley D. The Christian Teacher: Shepherds of Loving Kindness Don Bosco Publications, 2007

Some other books by Jim Gallagher

Serving the Young. *The religious dimension of education* Don Bosco Publications Bolton

Soil for the Seed: *Historical, Pastoral and Theological Reflections on Educating to and in the Faith* McCrimmon 2001

Our Schools our faith Collins 1988

Guidelines Collins 1986

Printed in Great Britain
by Amazon.co.uk, Ltd.,
Marston Gate.